Beautiful Women Colouring book

Thank you for selecting this colouring book.
We work hard to give you original ccolour books for people for all ages.
If you like this colouring book kindly consider a review.
Your review are sale booster and it allows us to produce more content for your delight.
Many thanks and Have fun colouring.

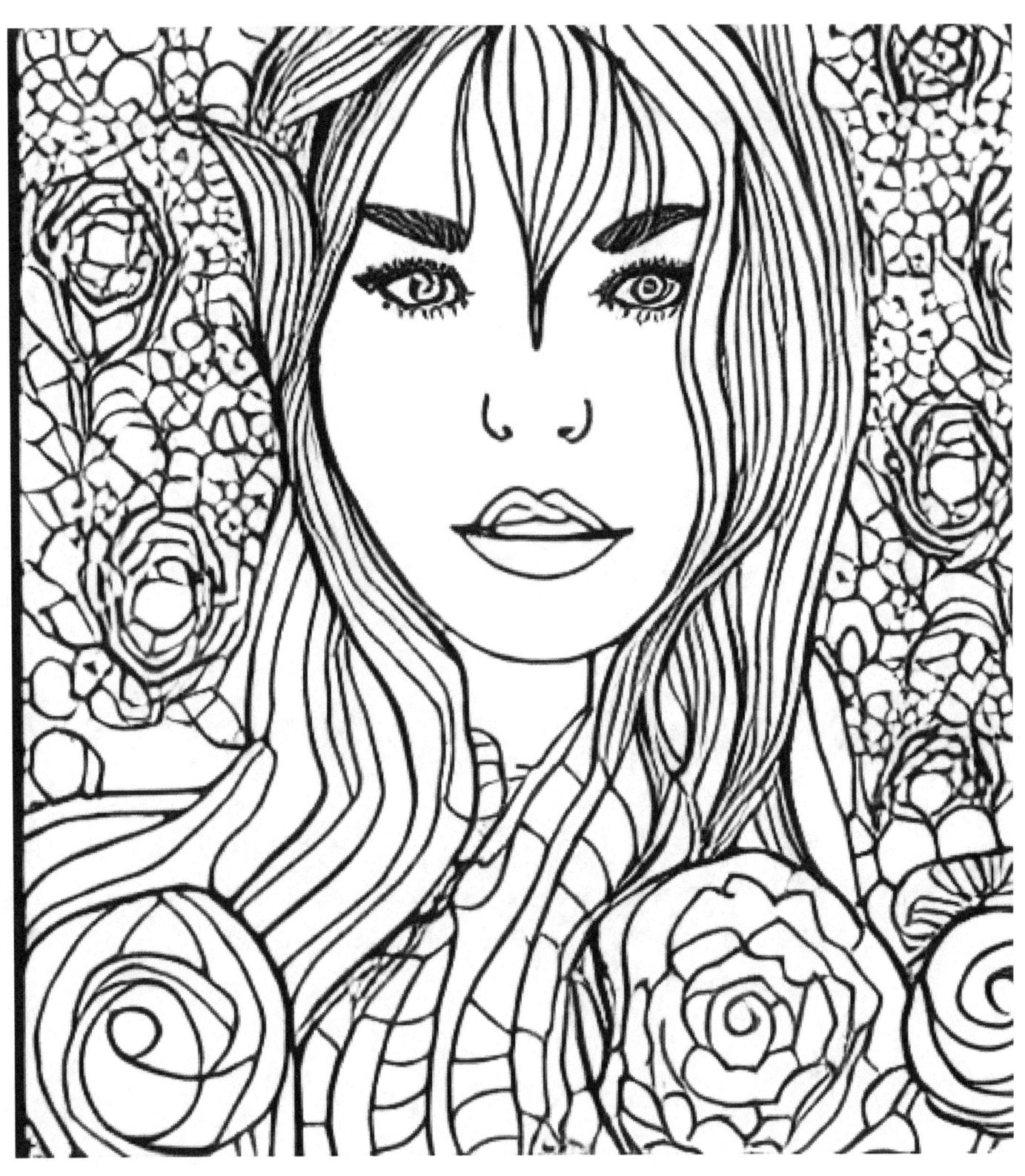

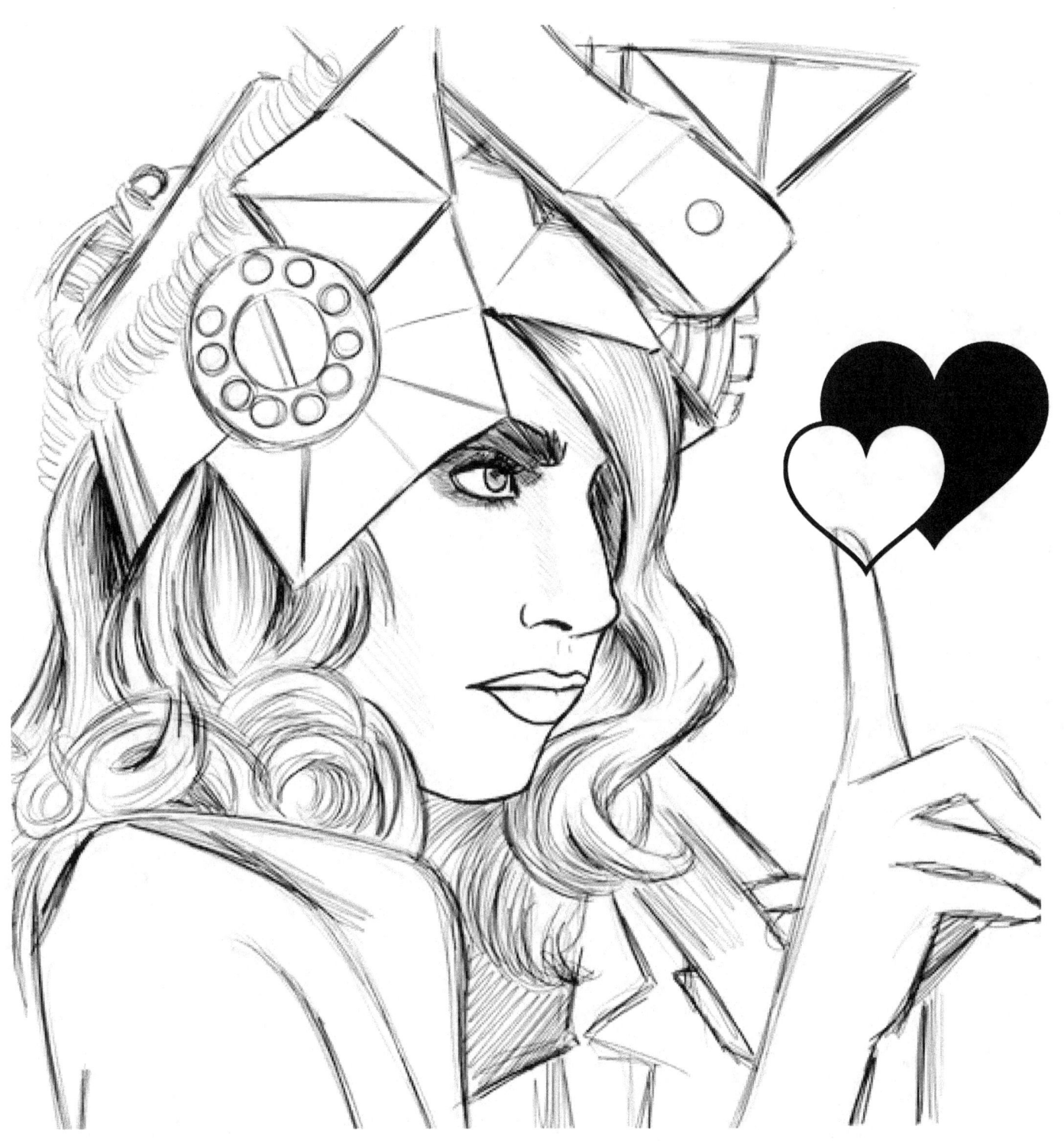

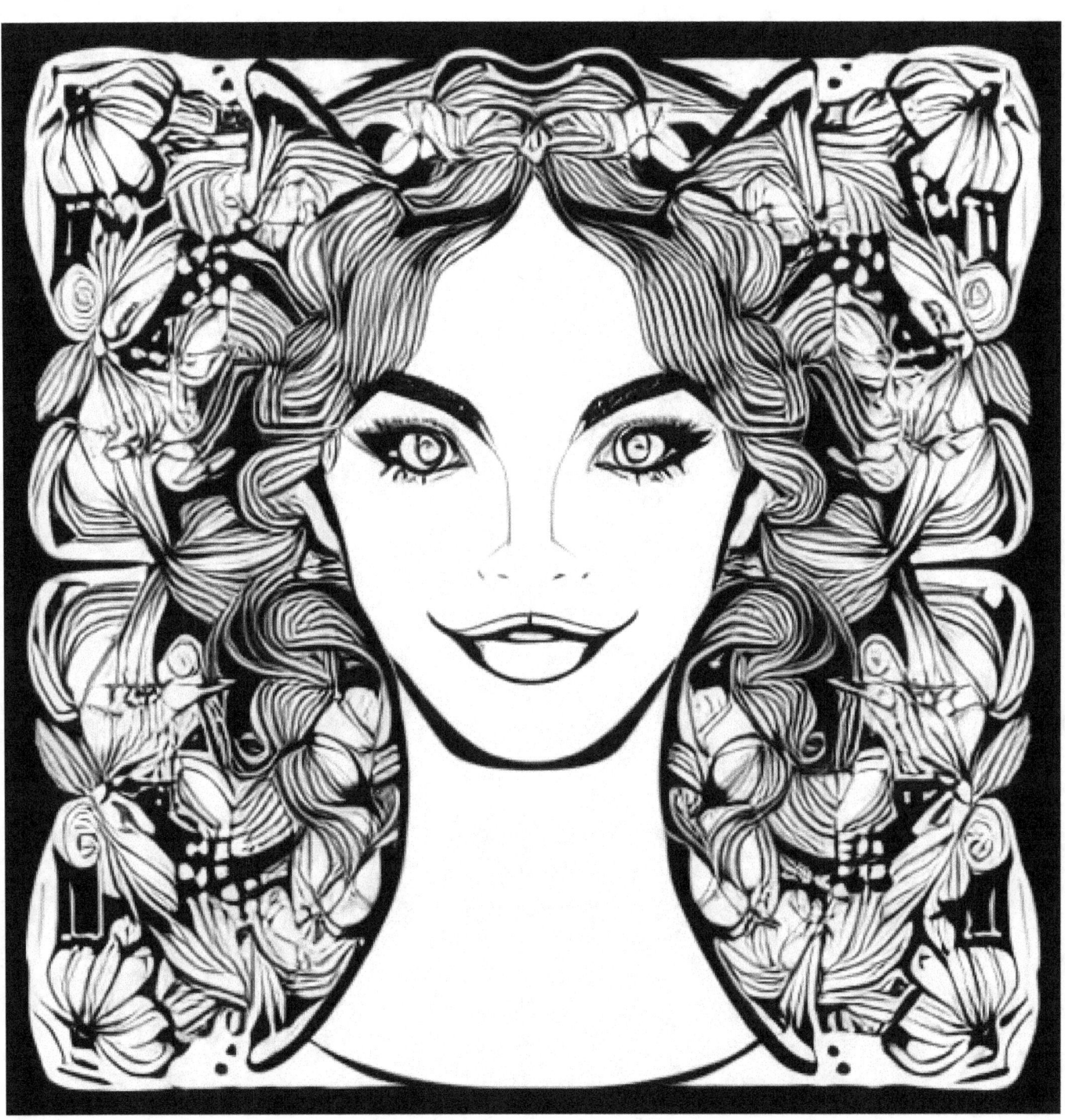

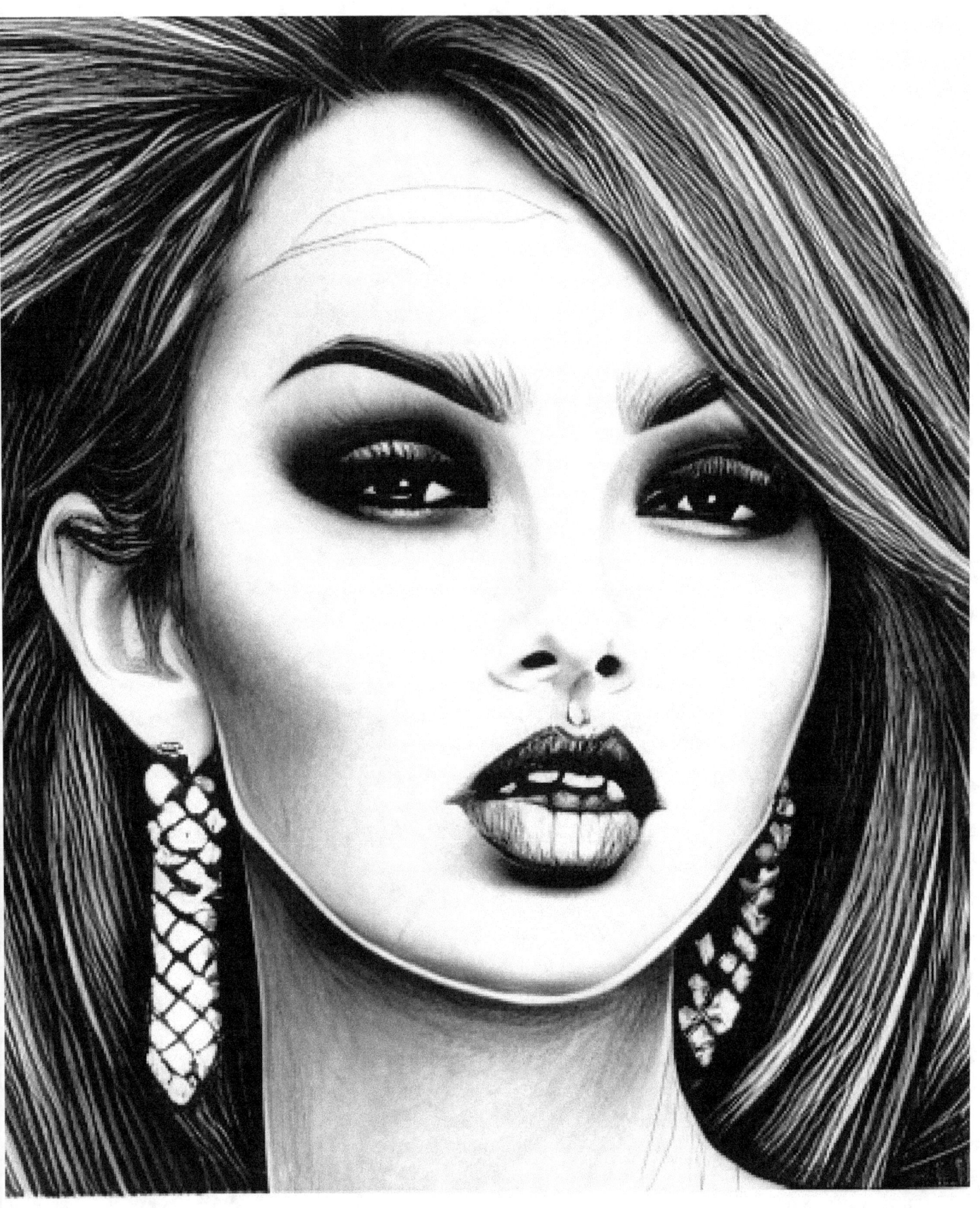

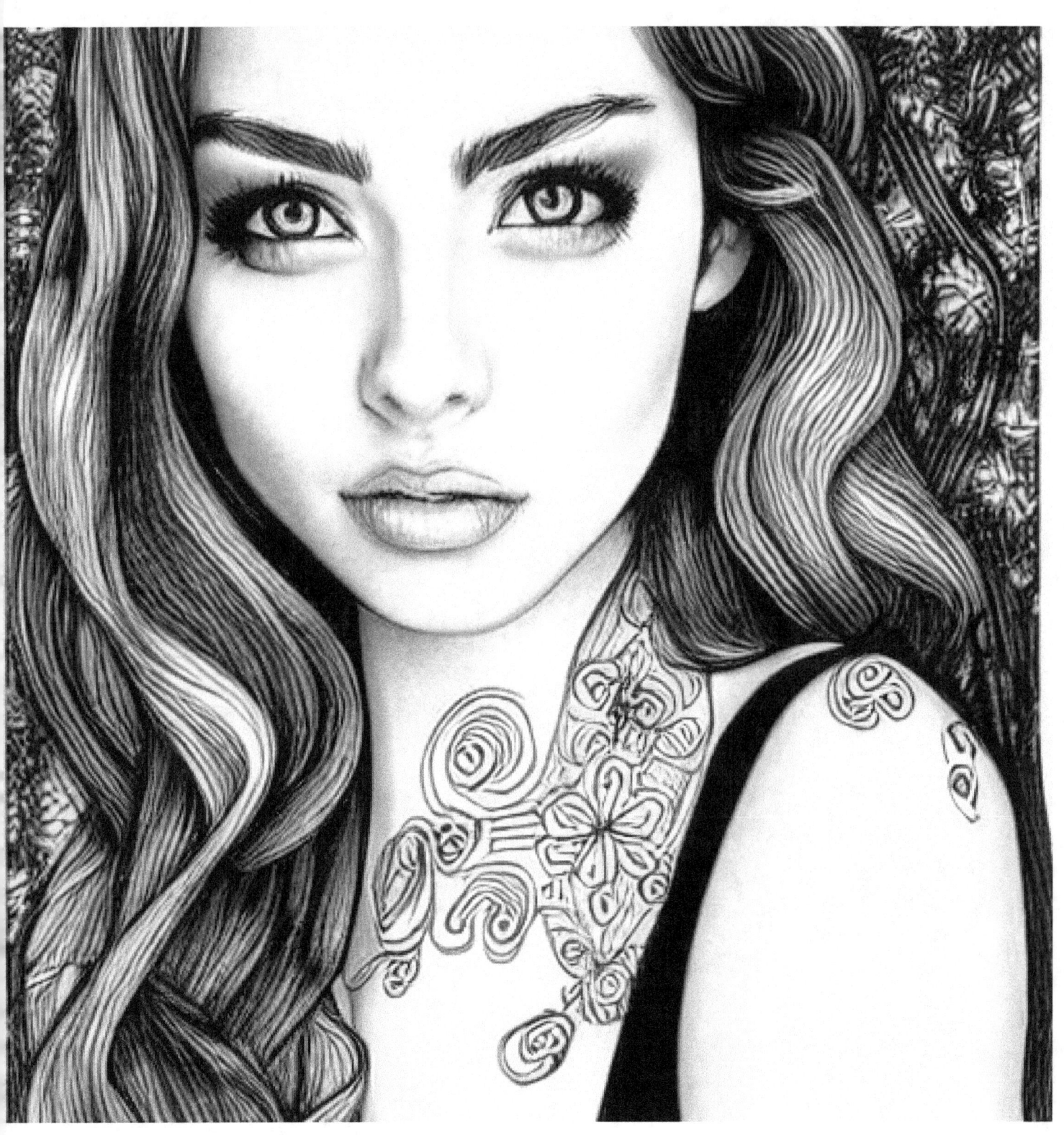

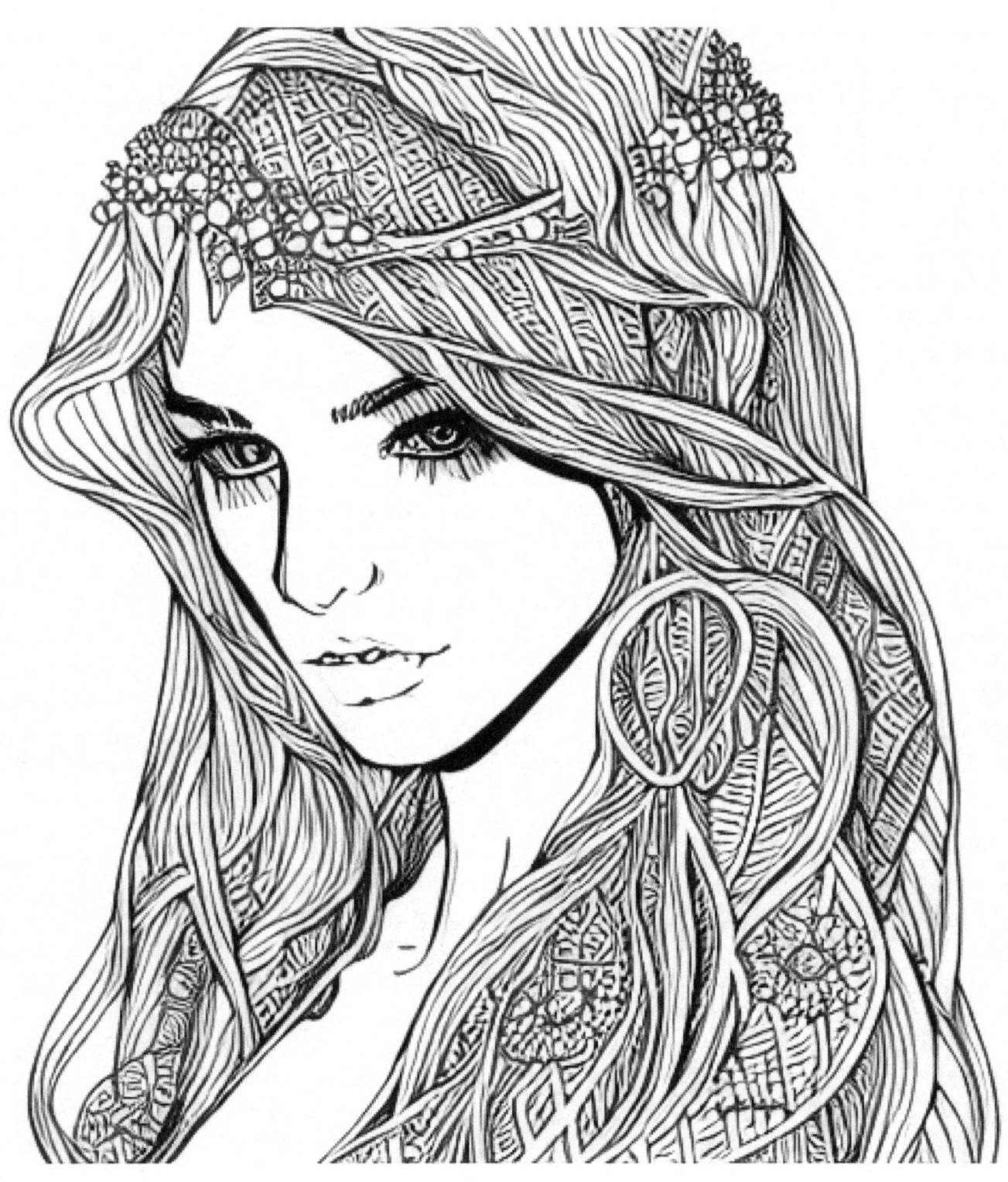

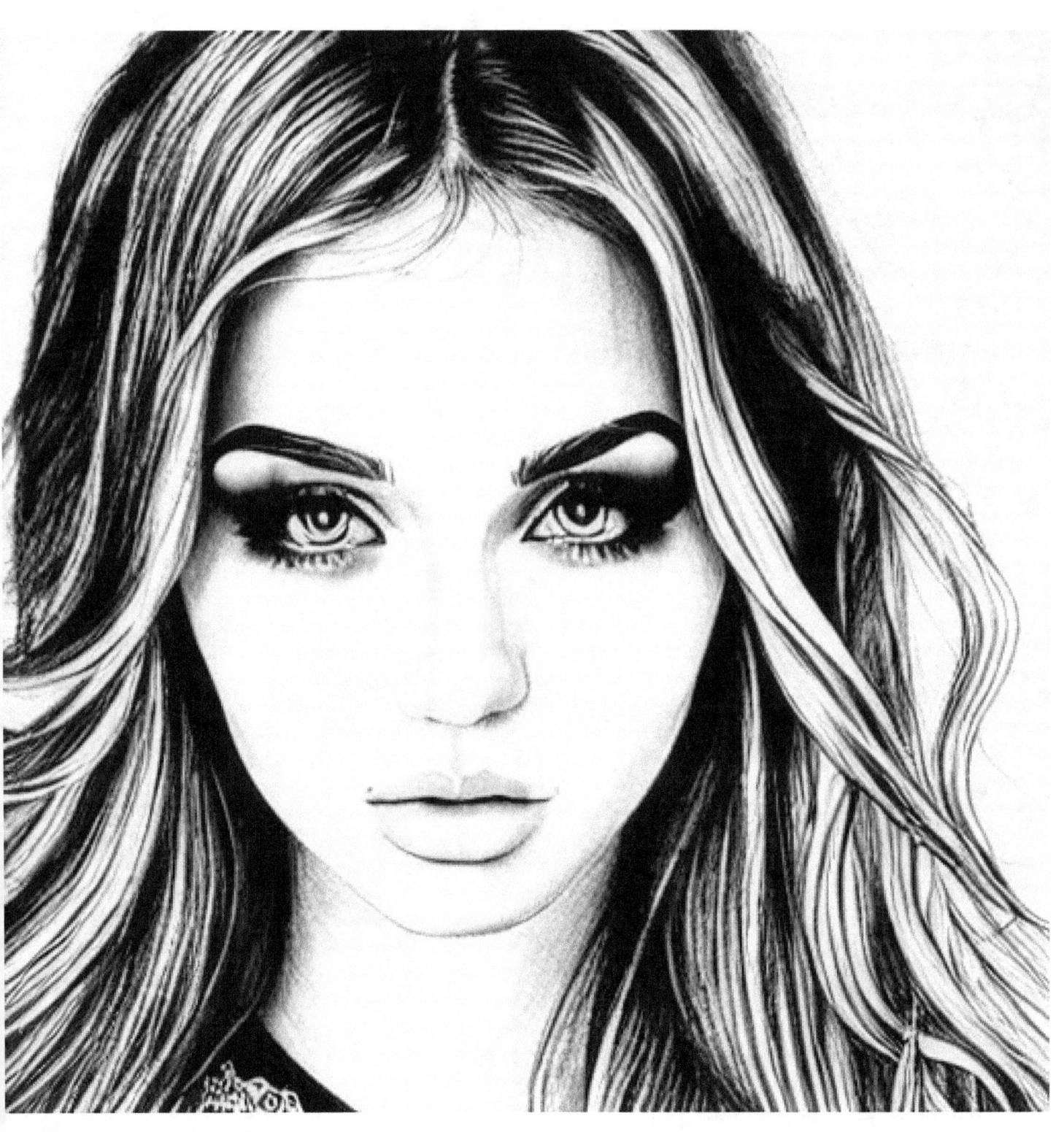

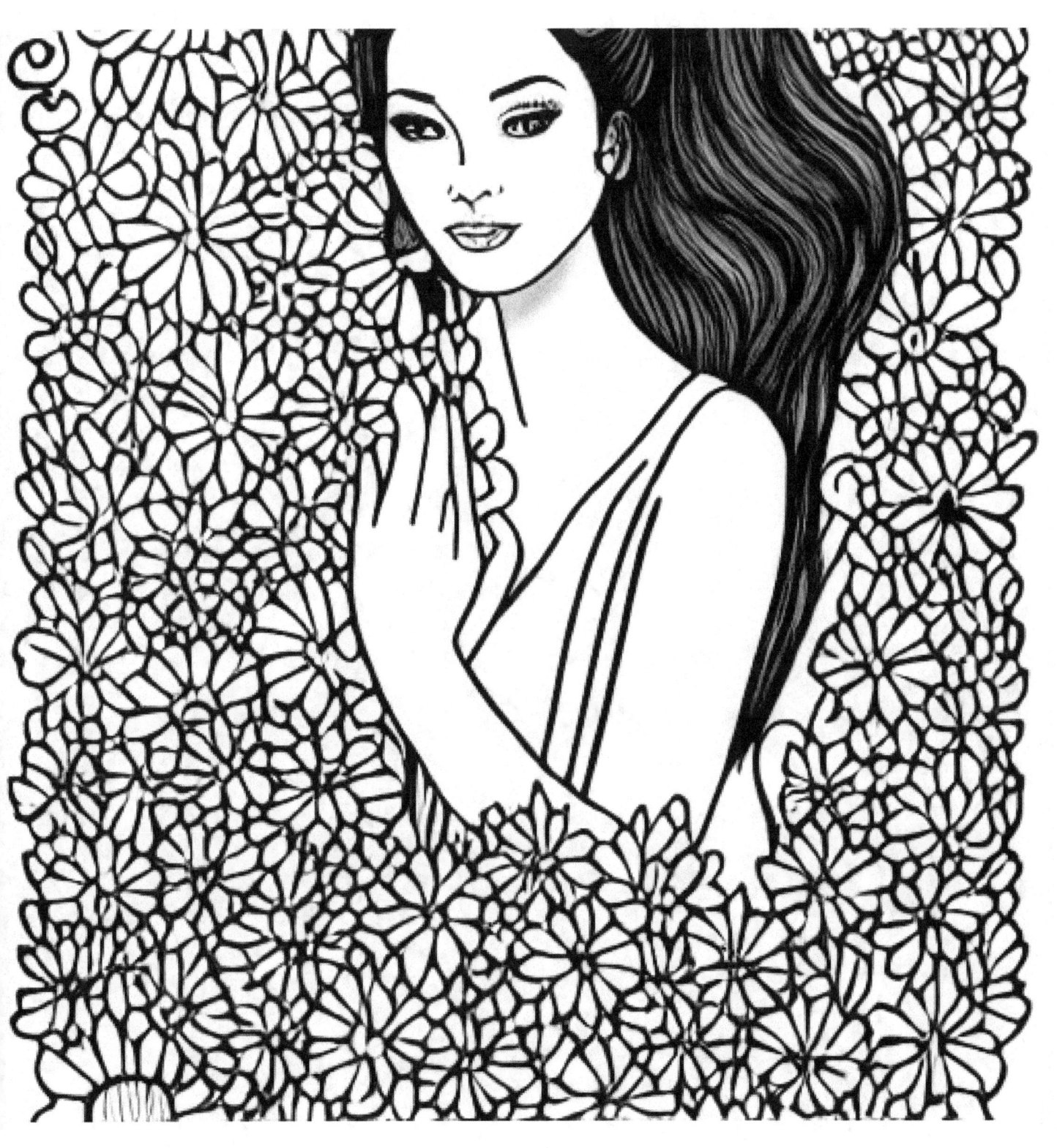

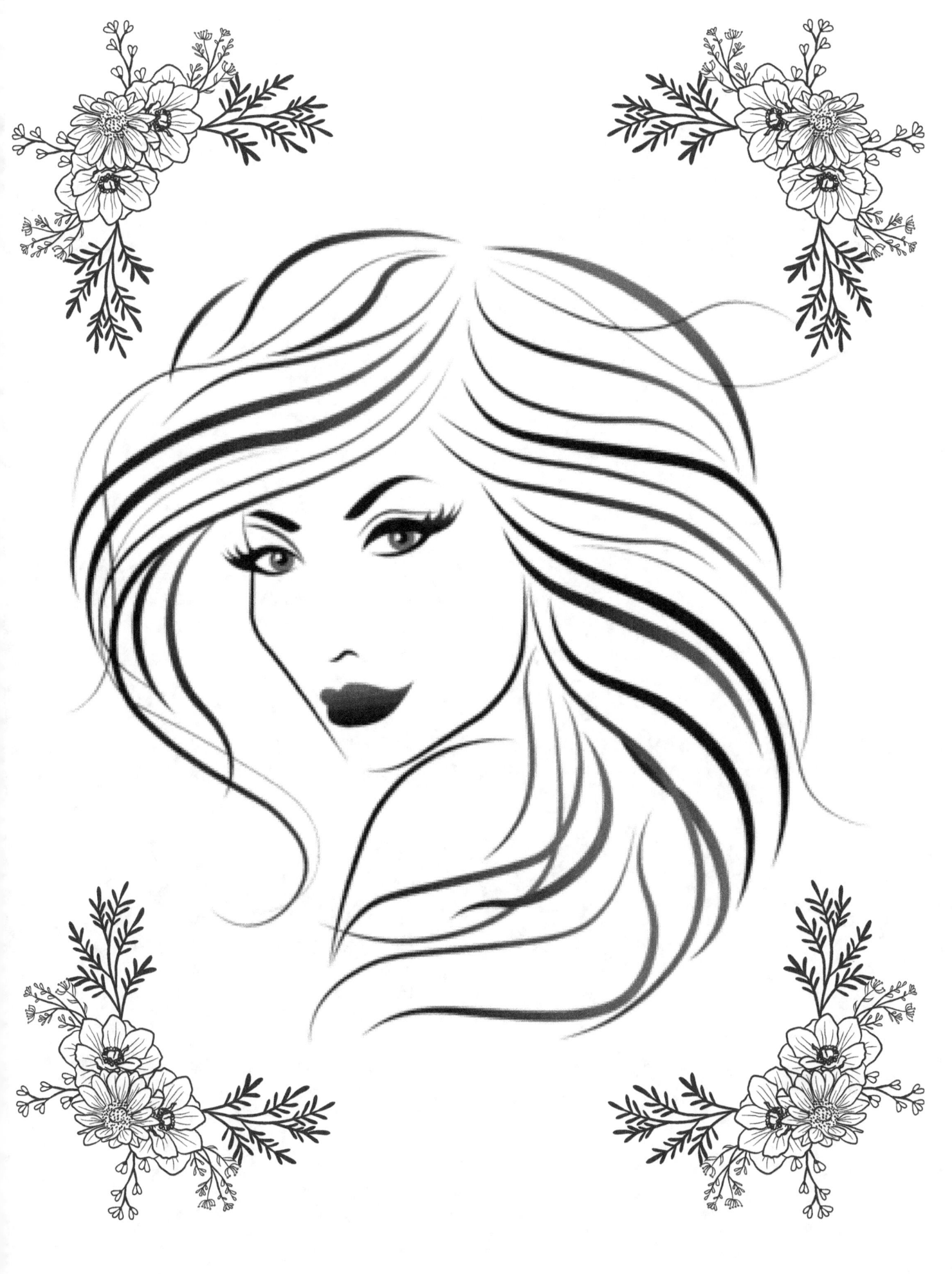

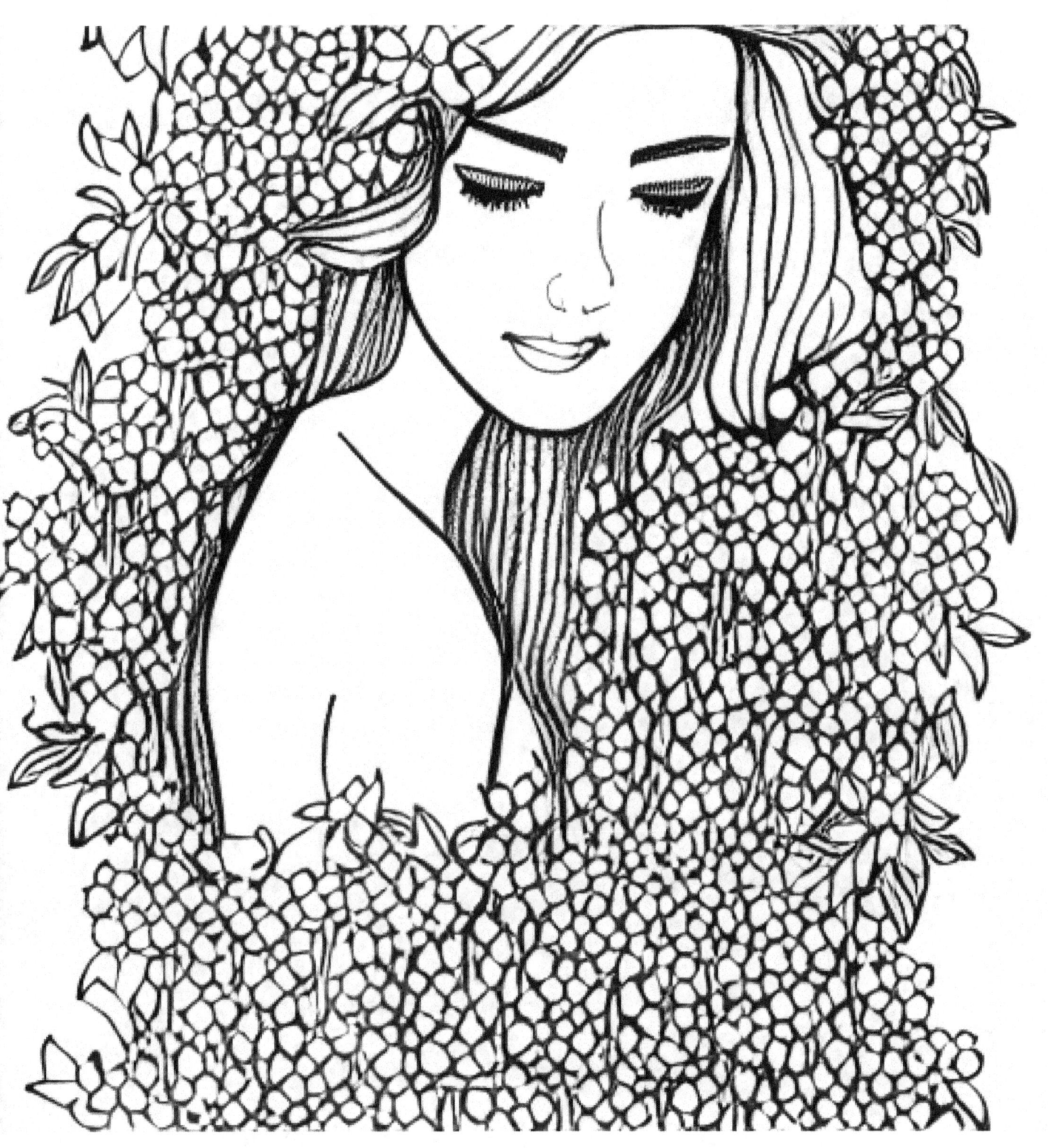

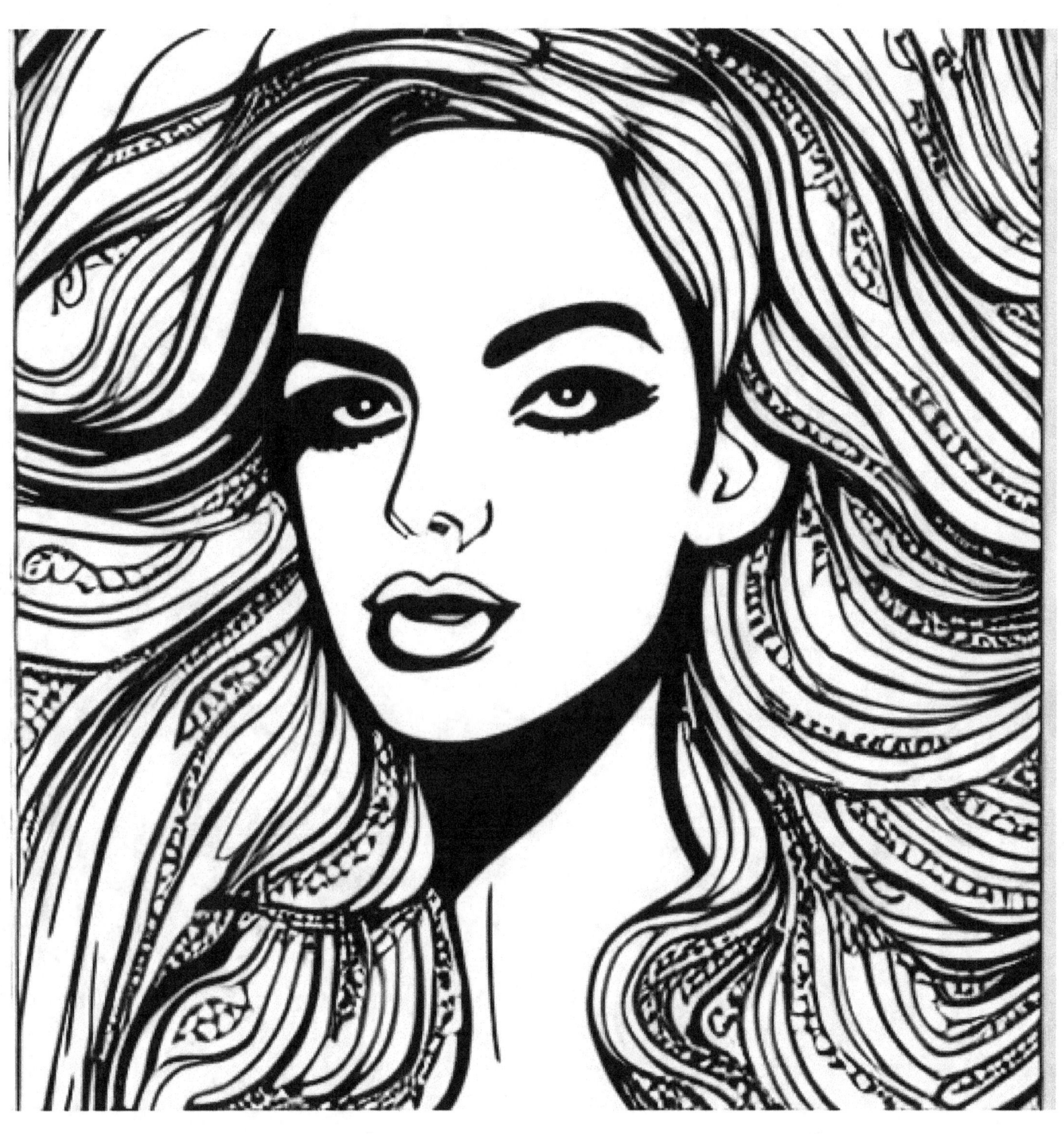

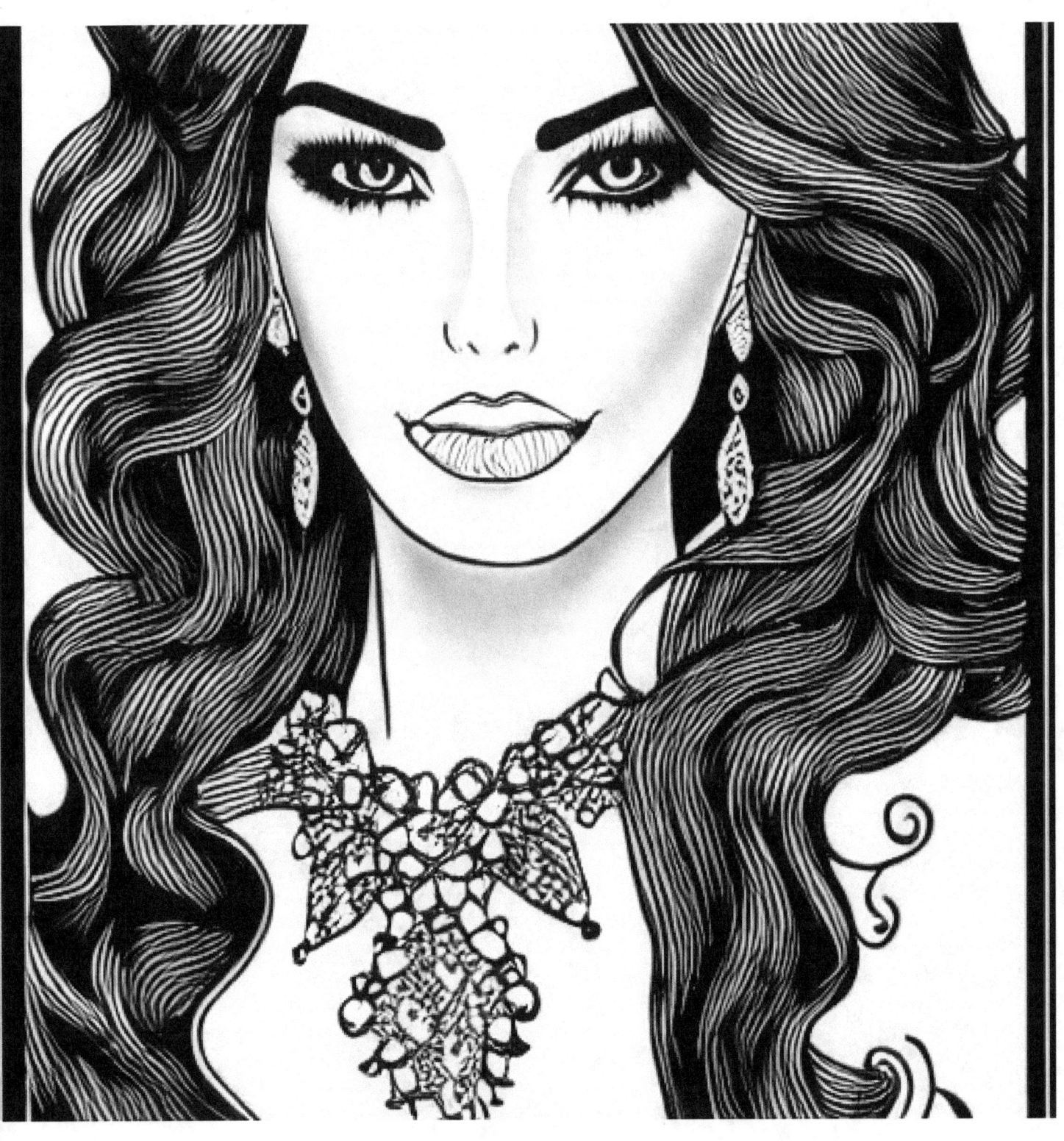

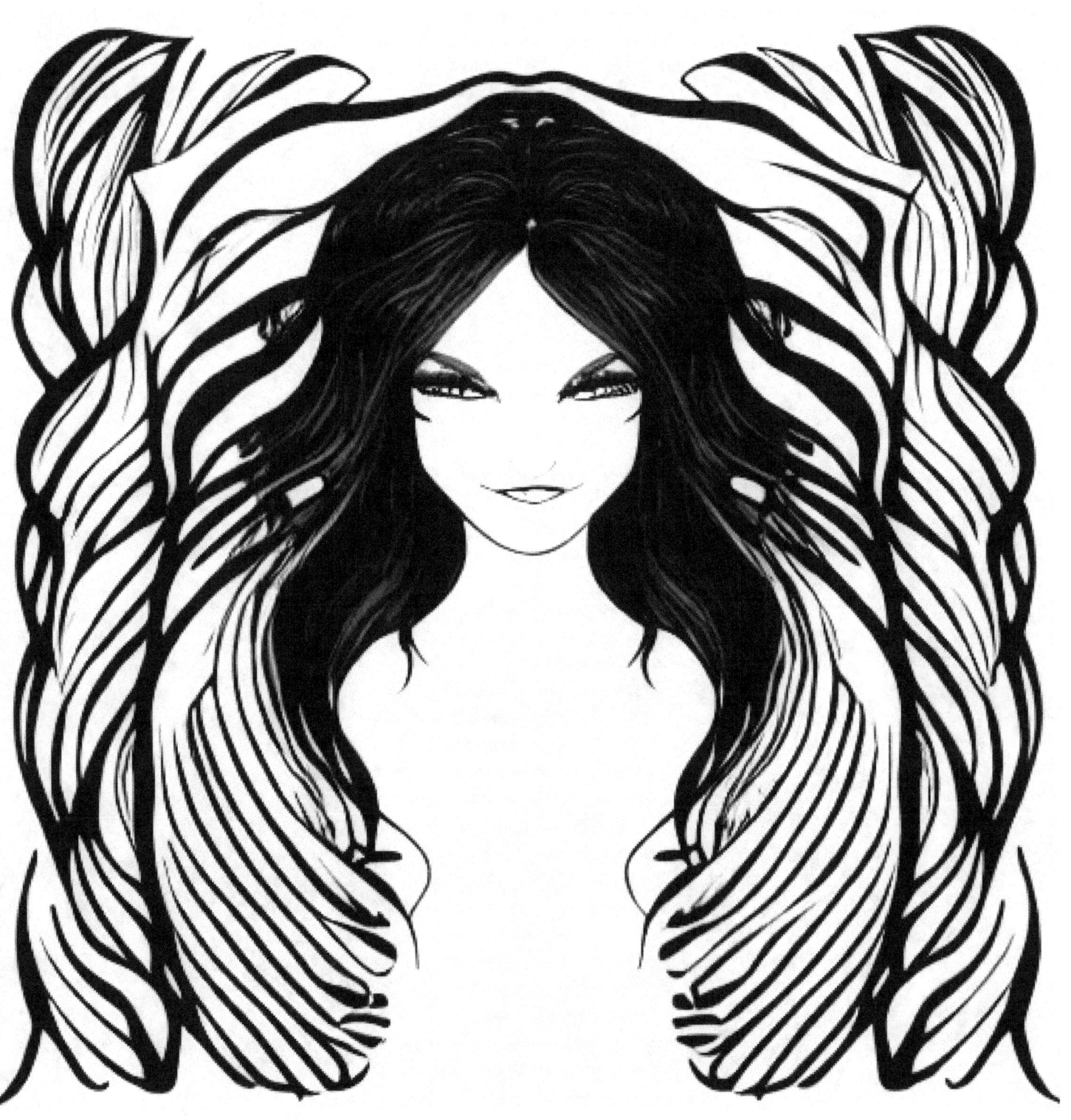

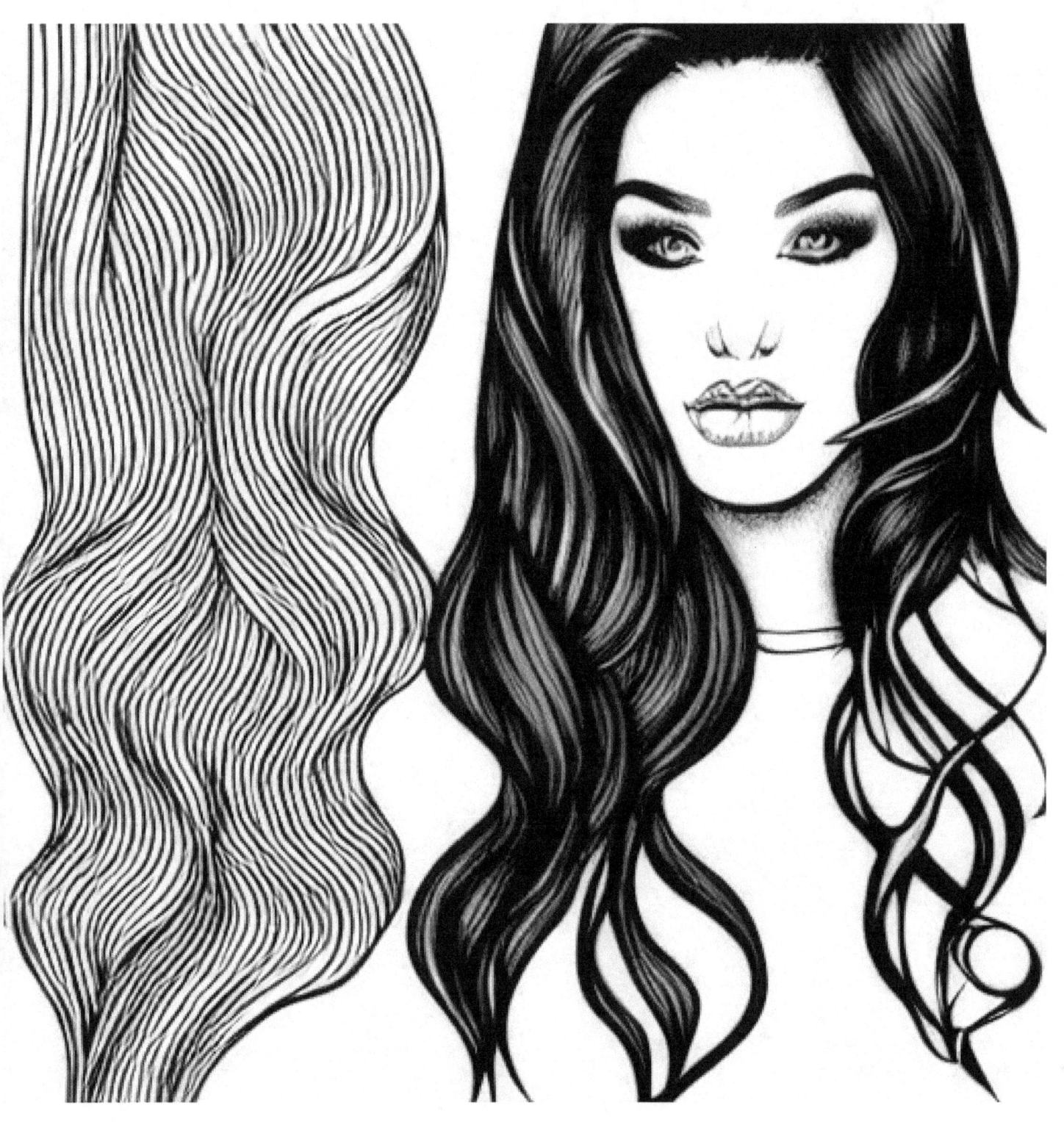

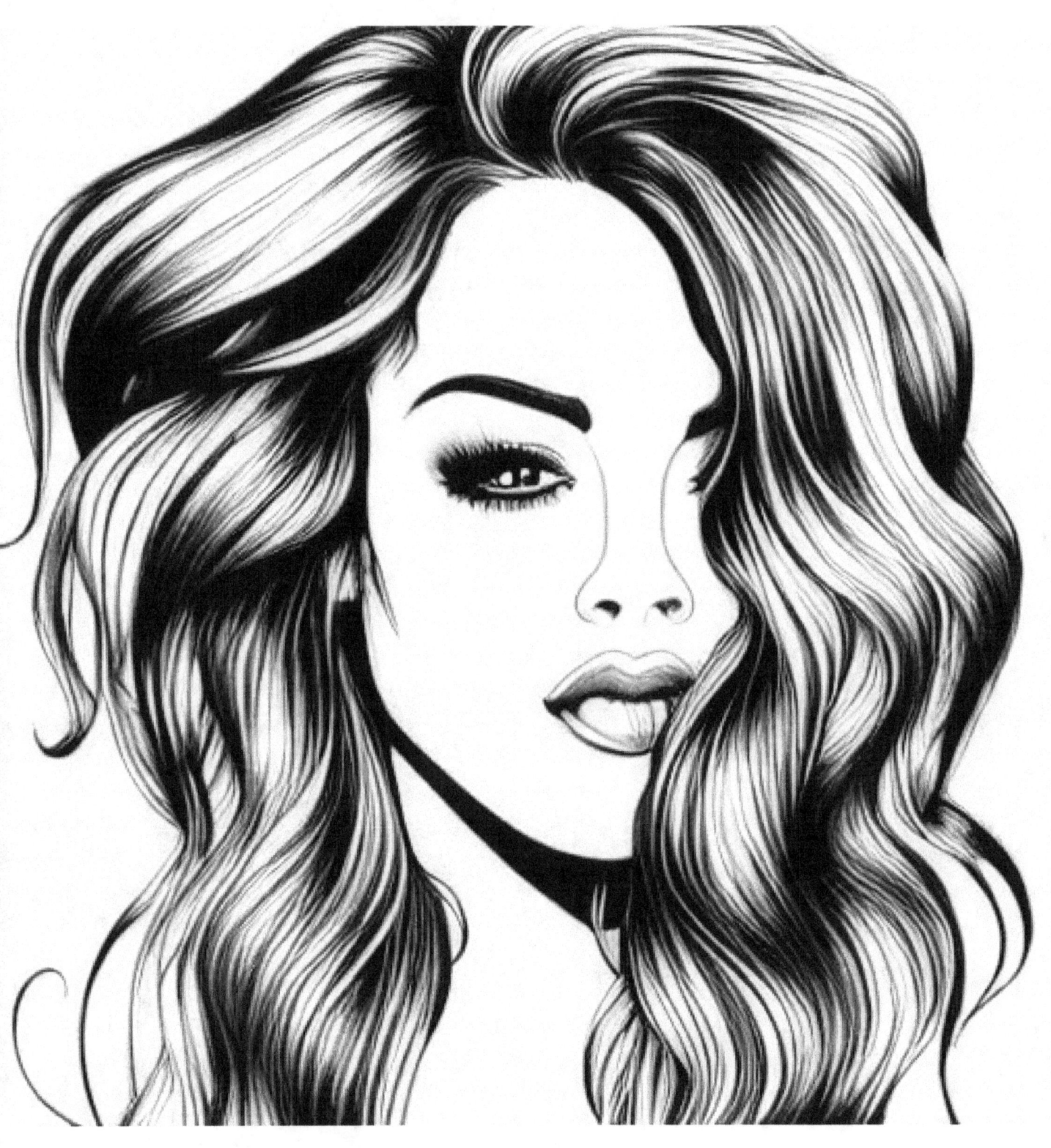

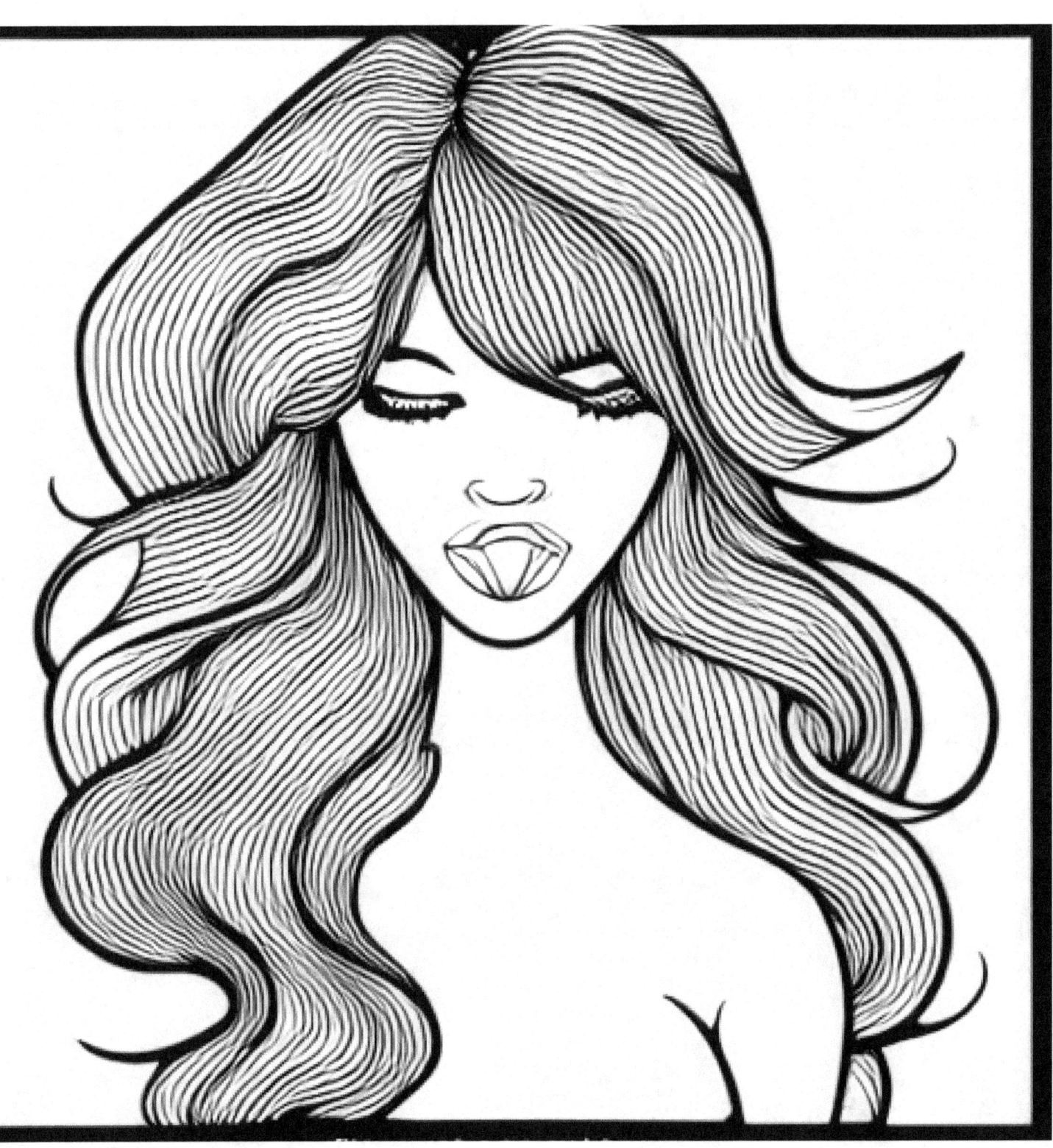

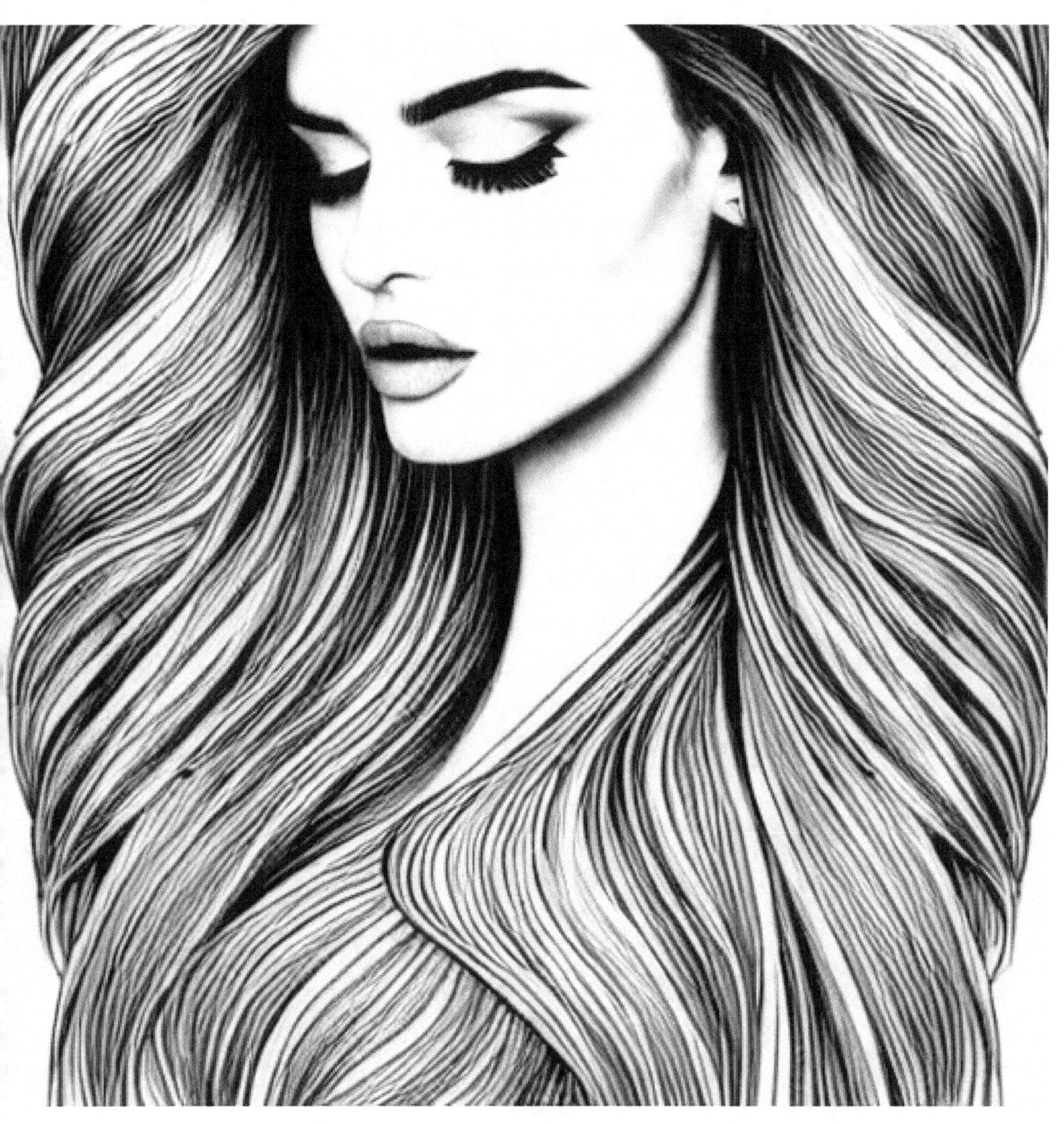

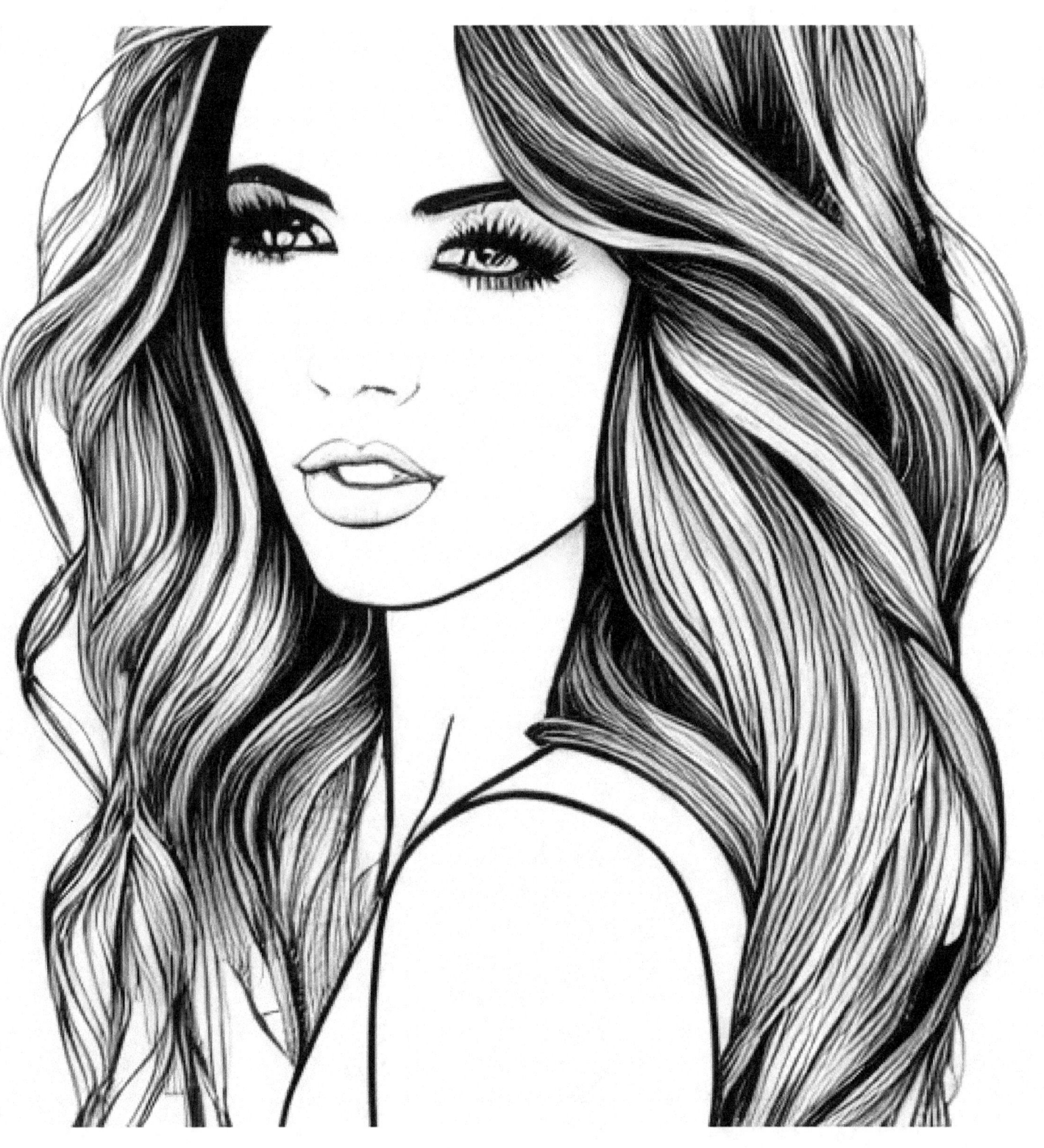

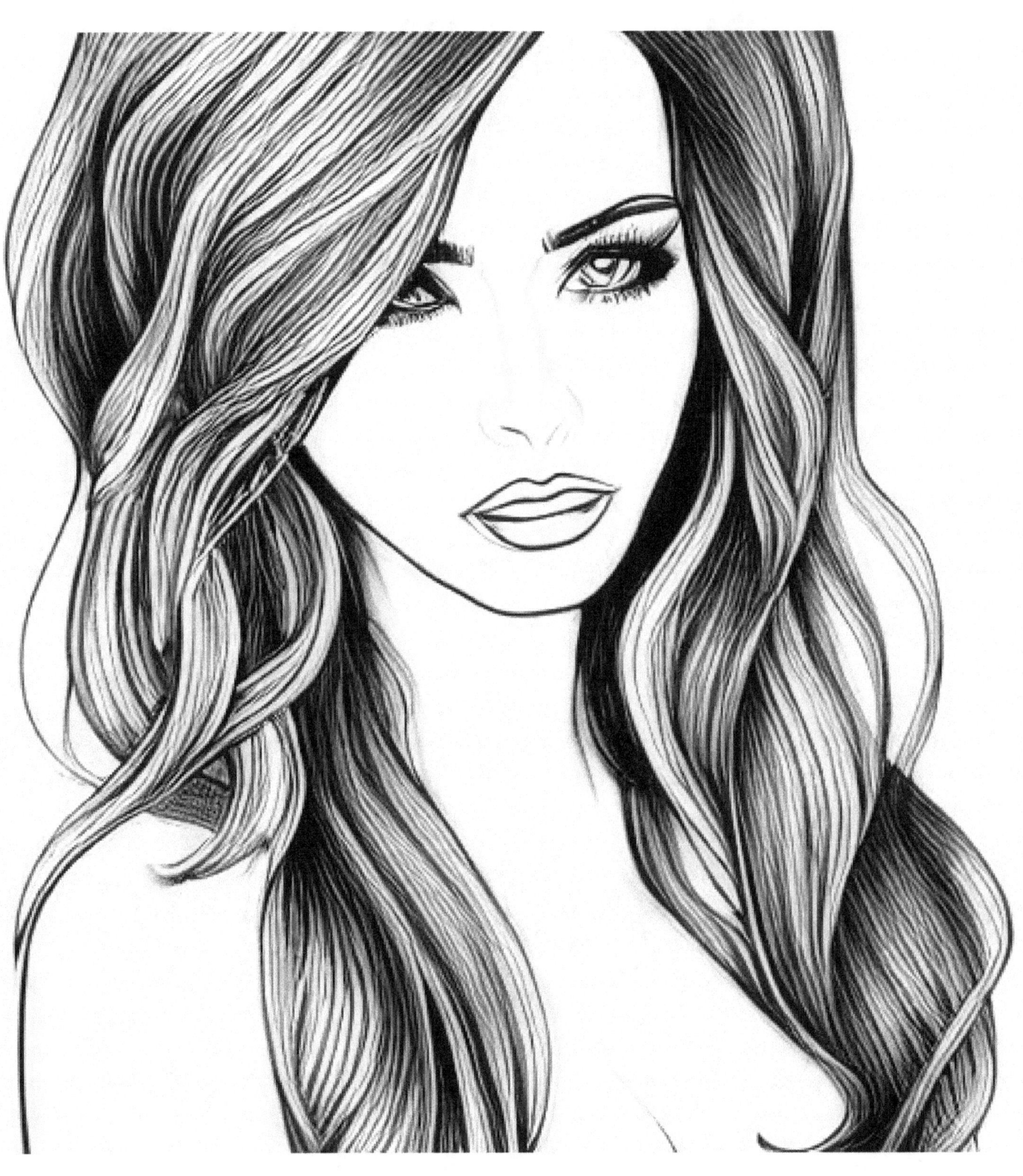

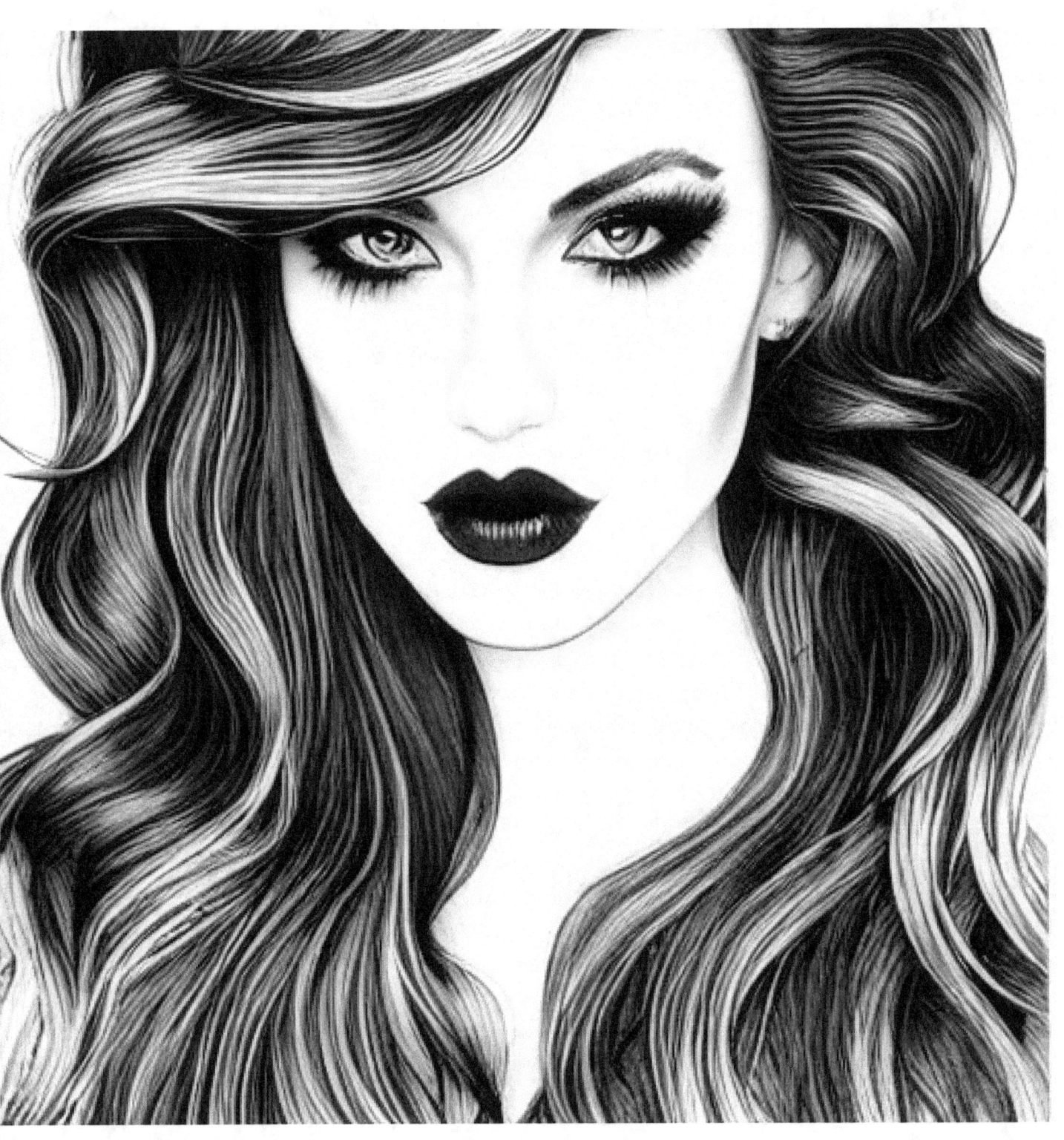

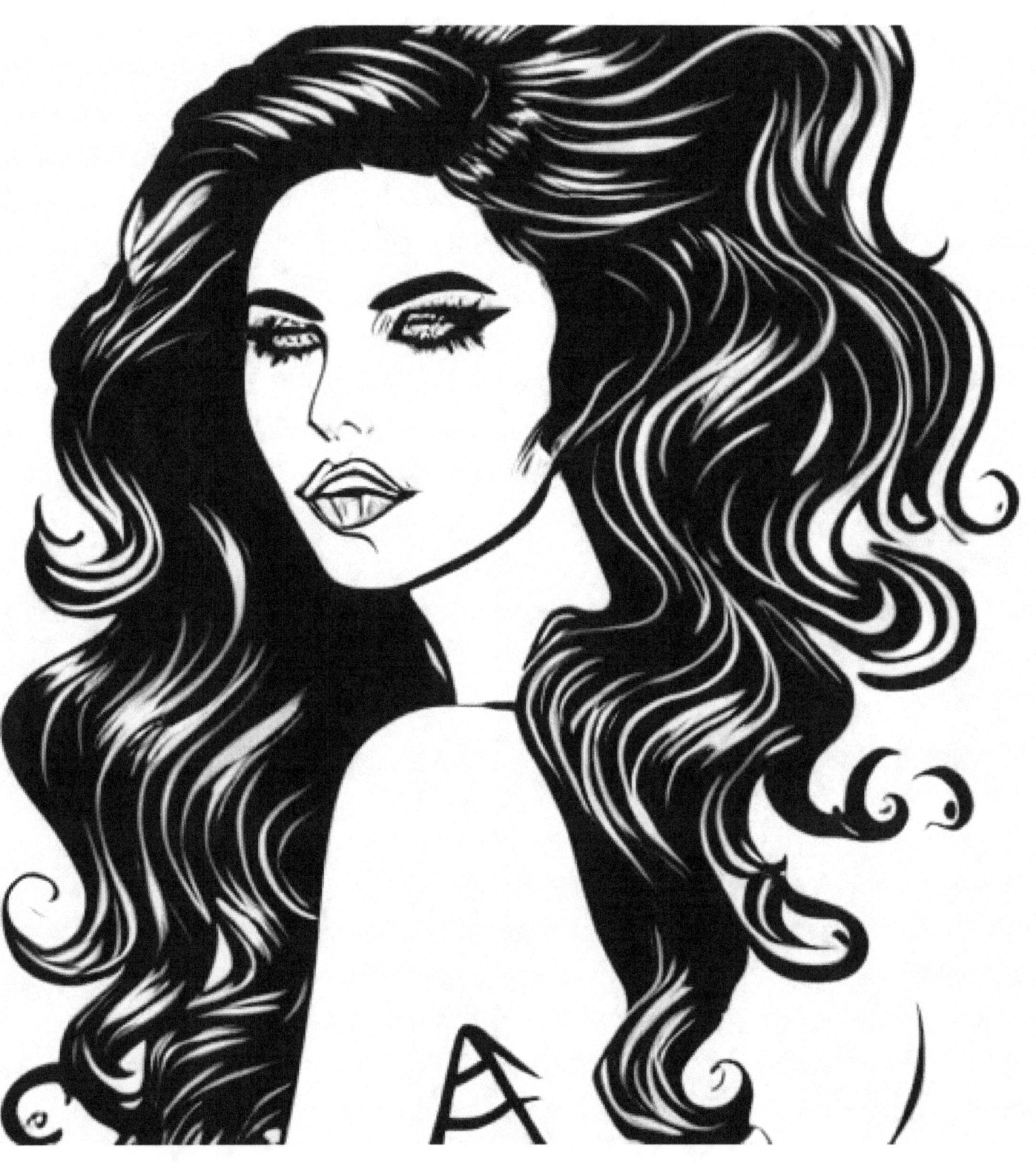

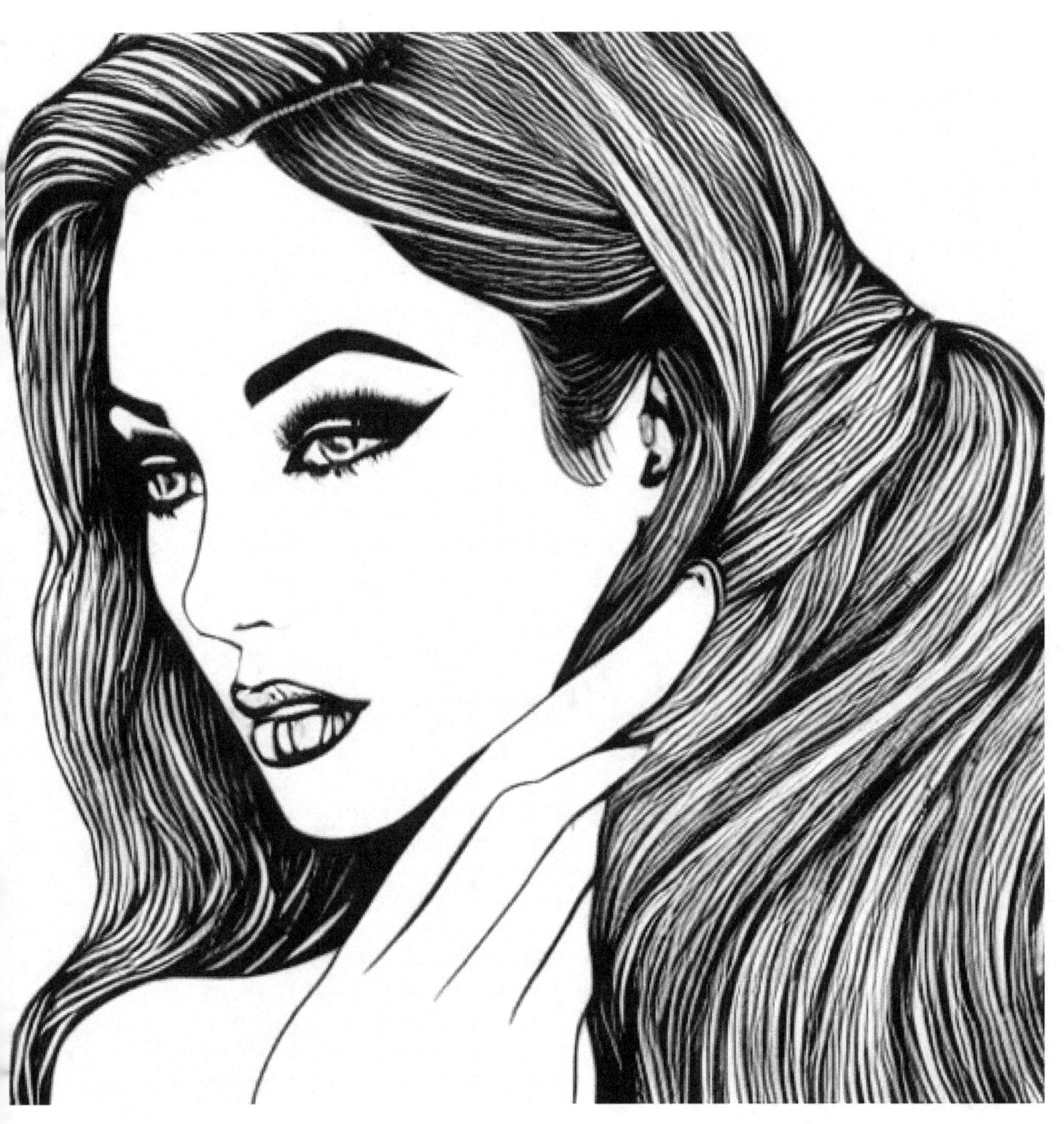

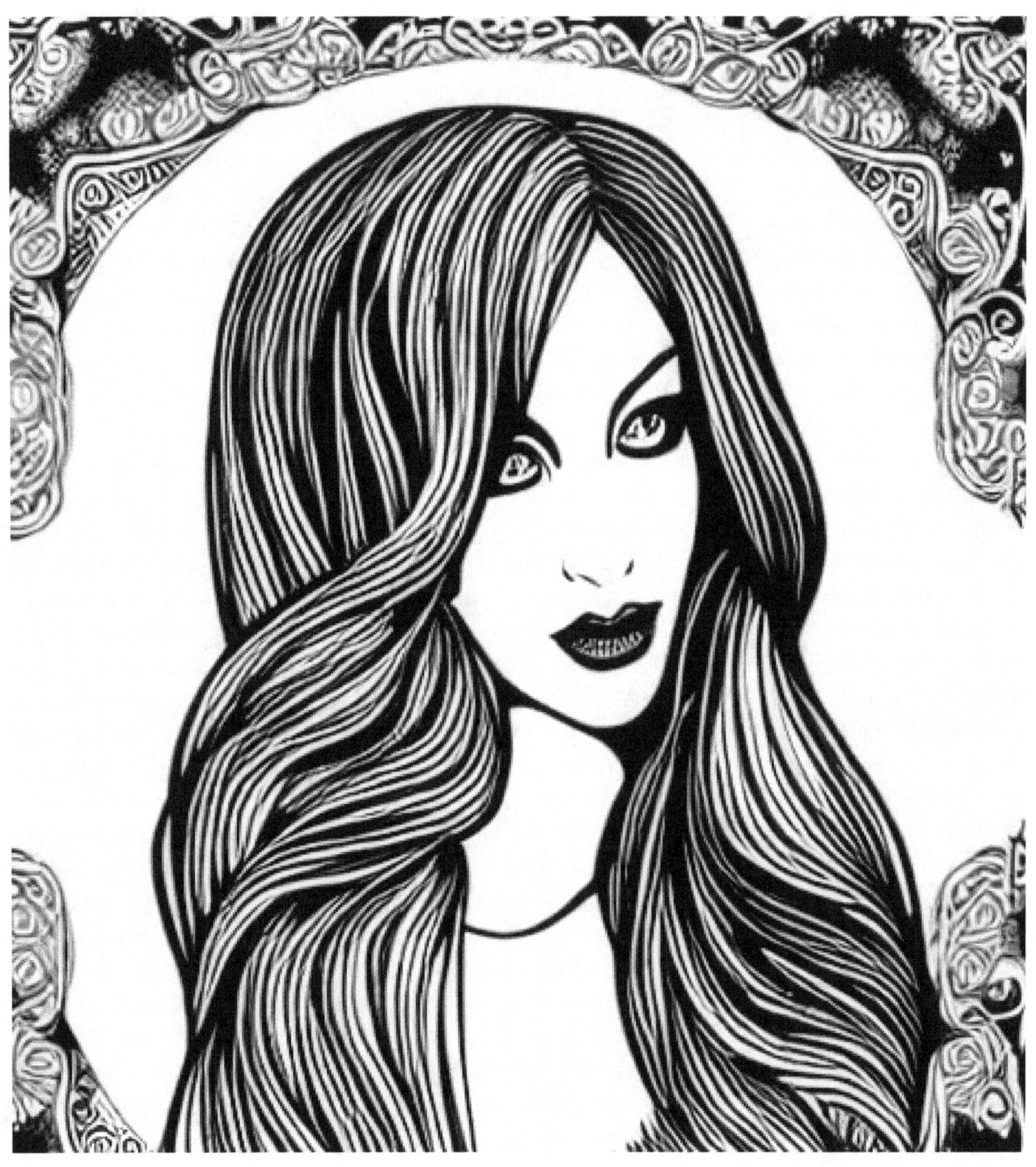

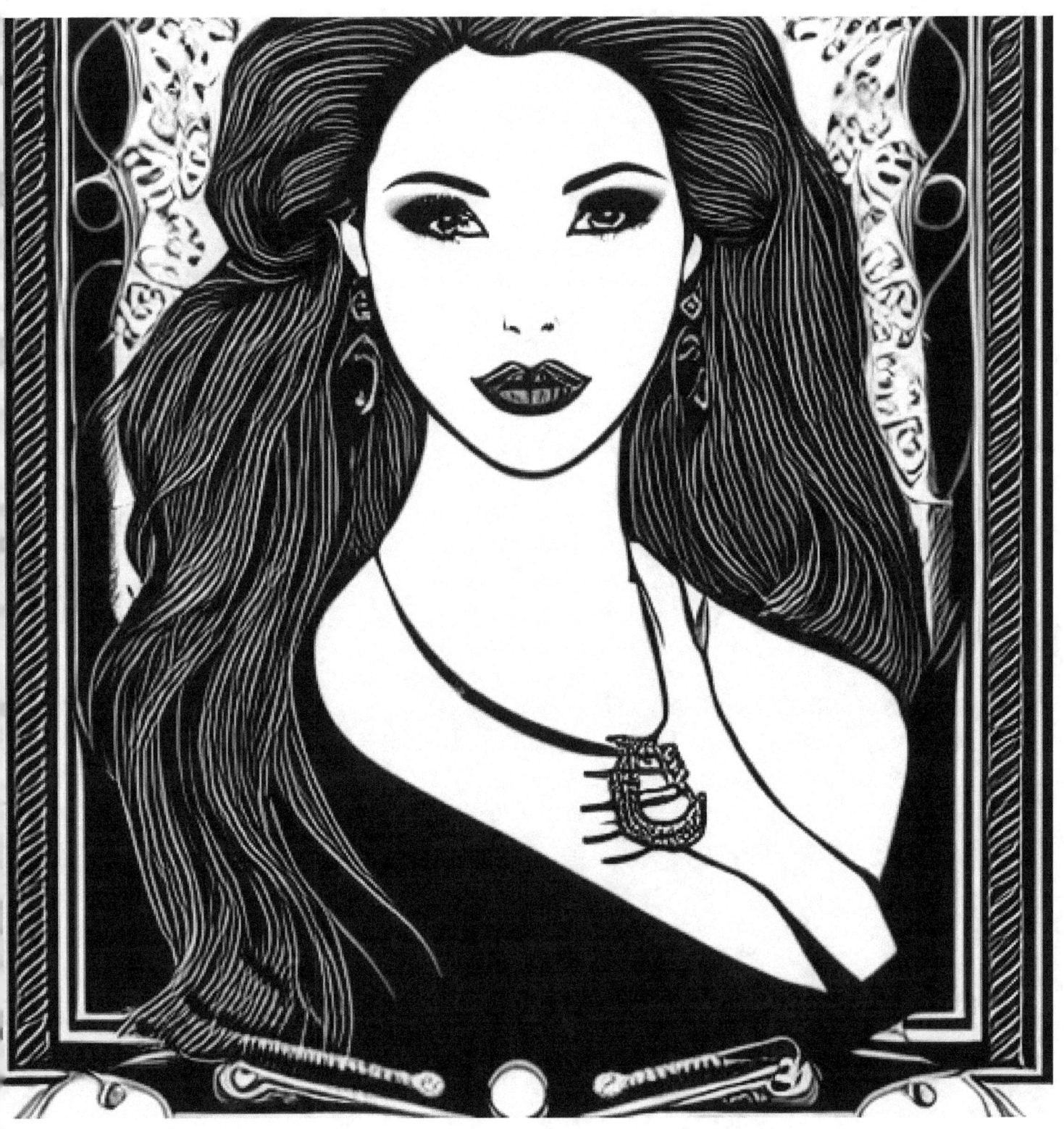

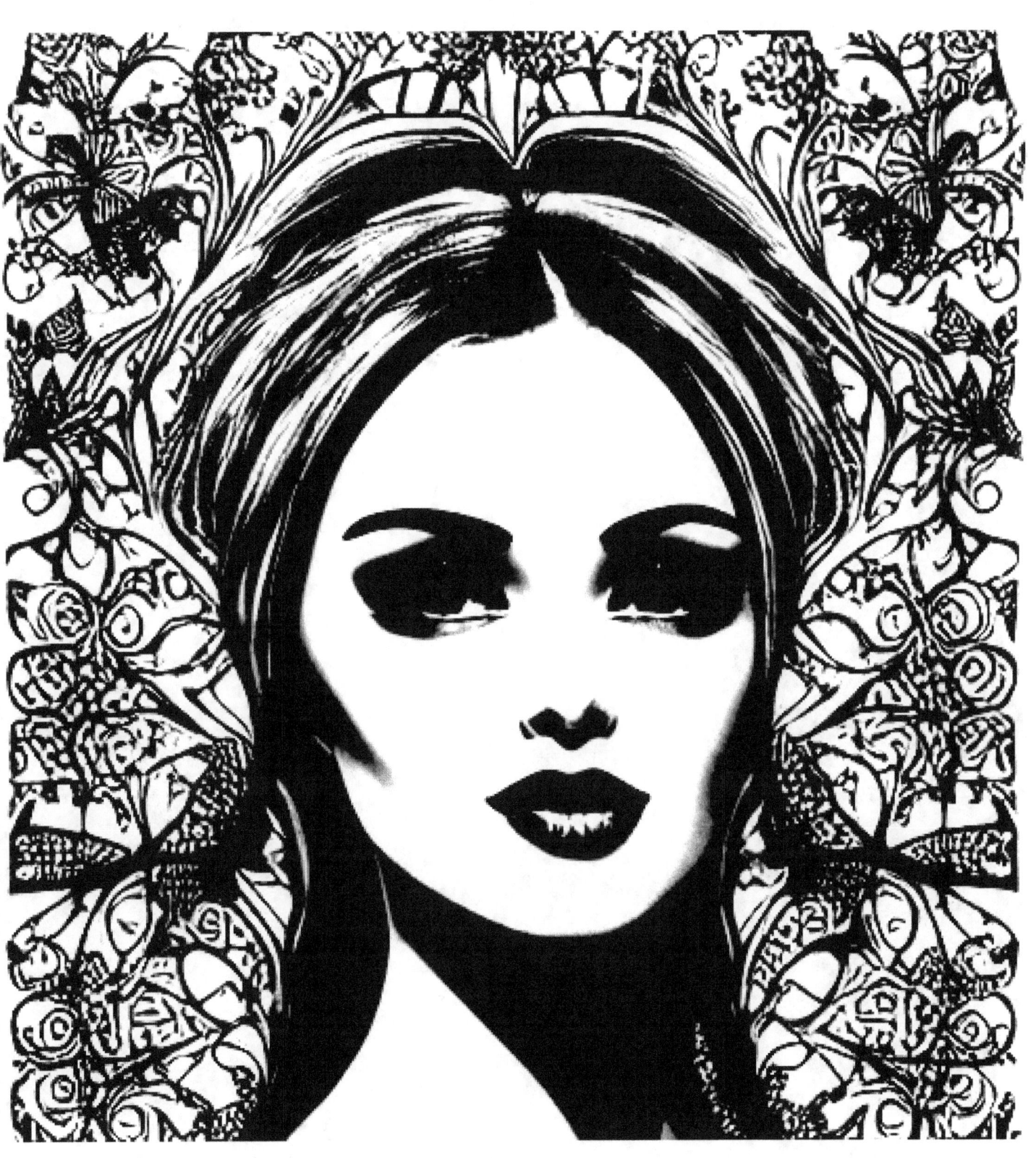

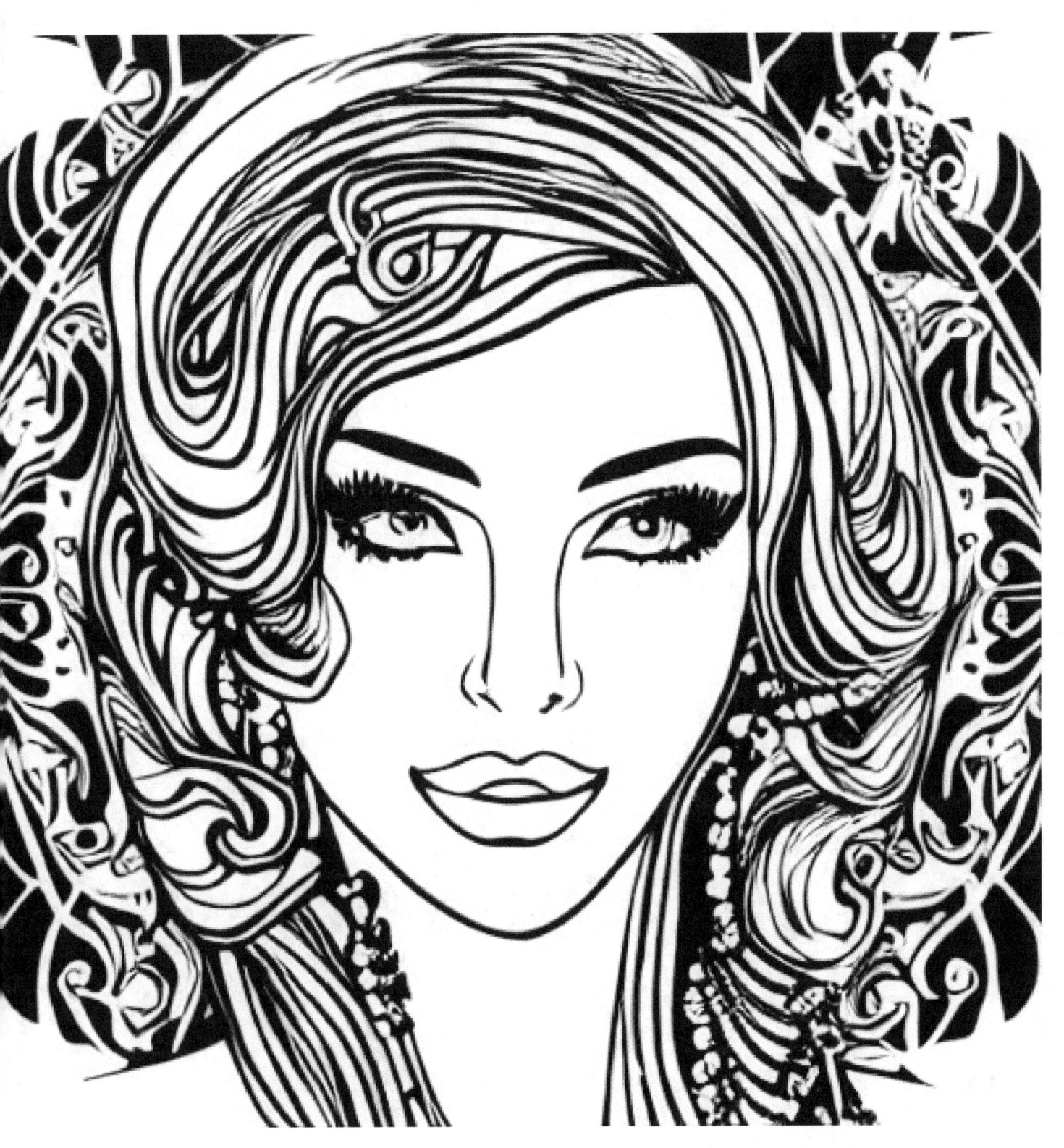

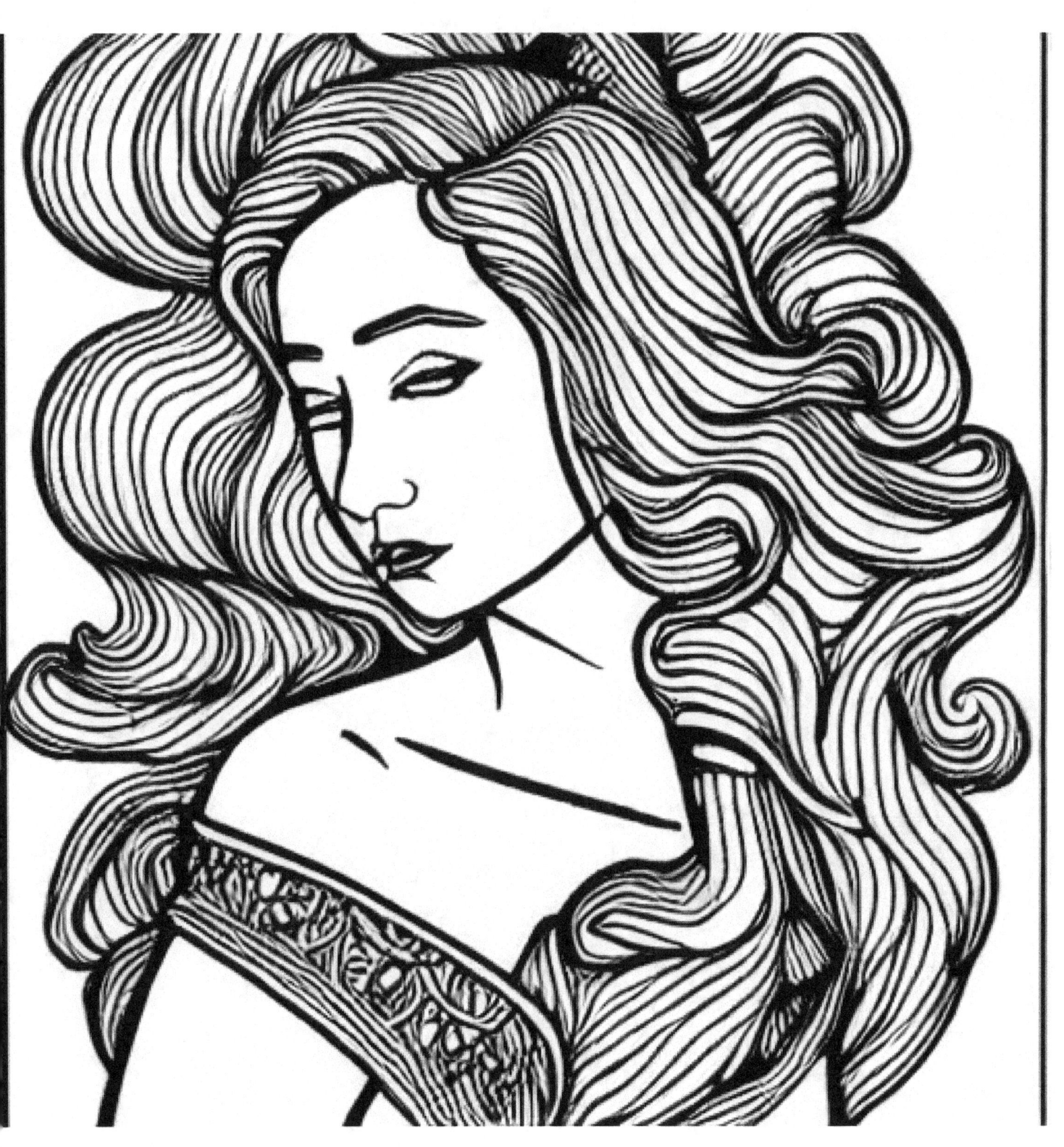

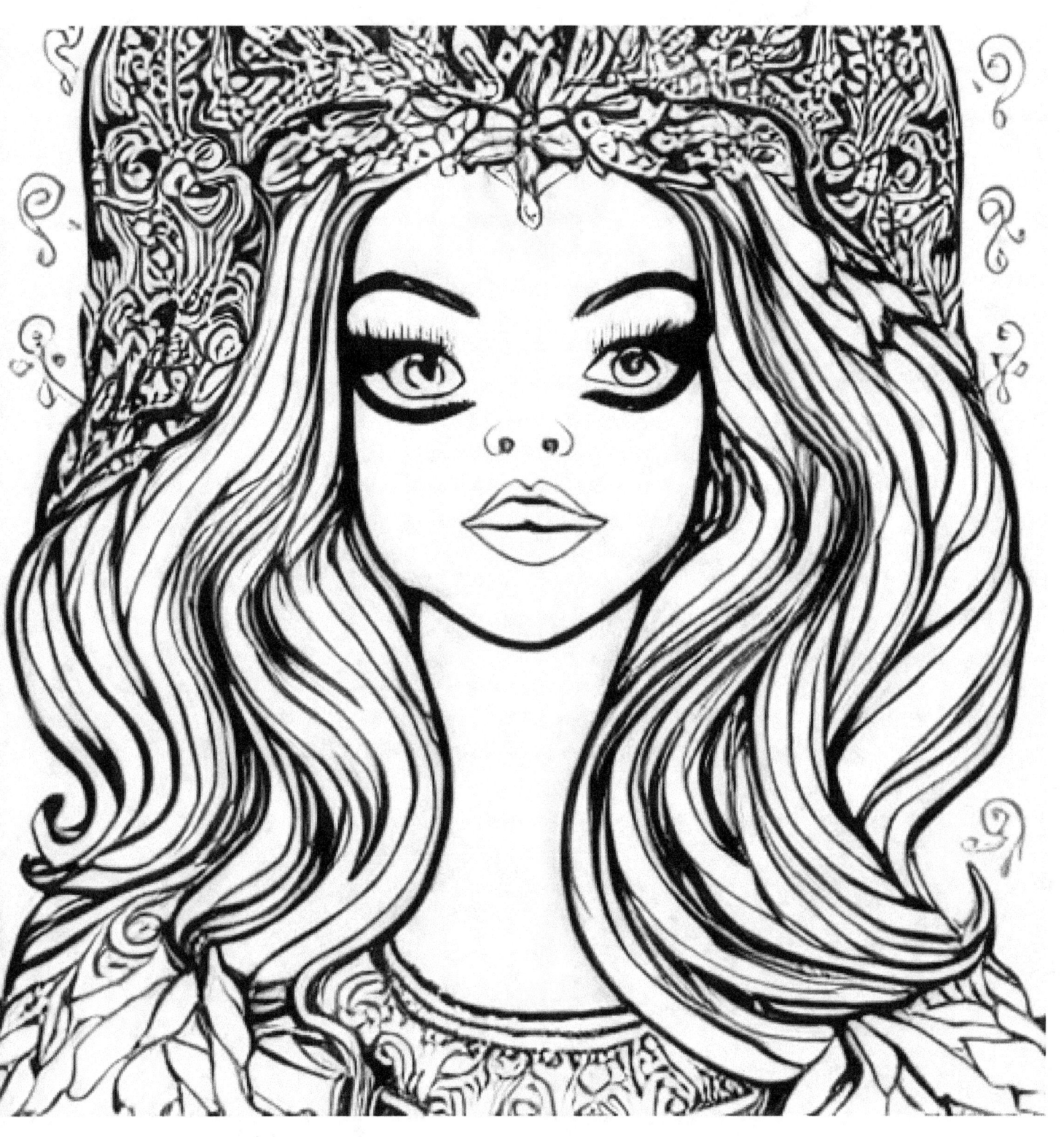

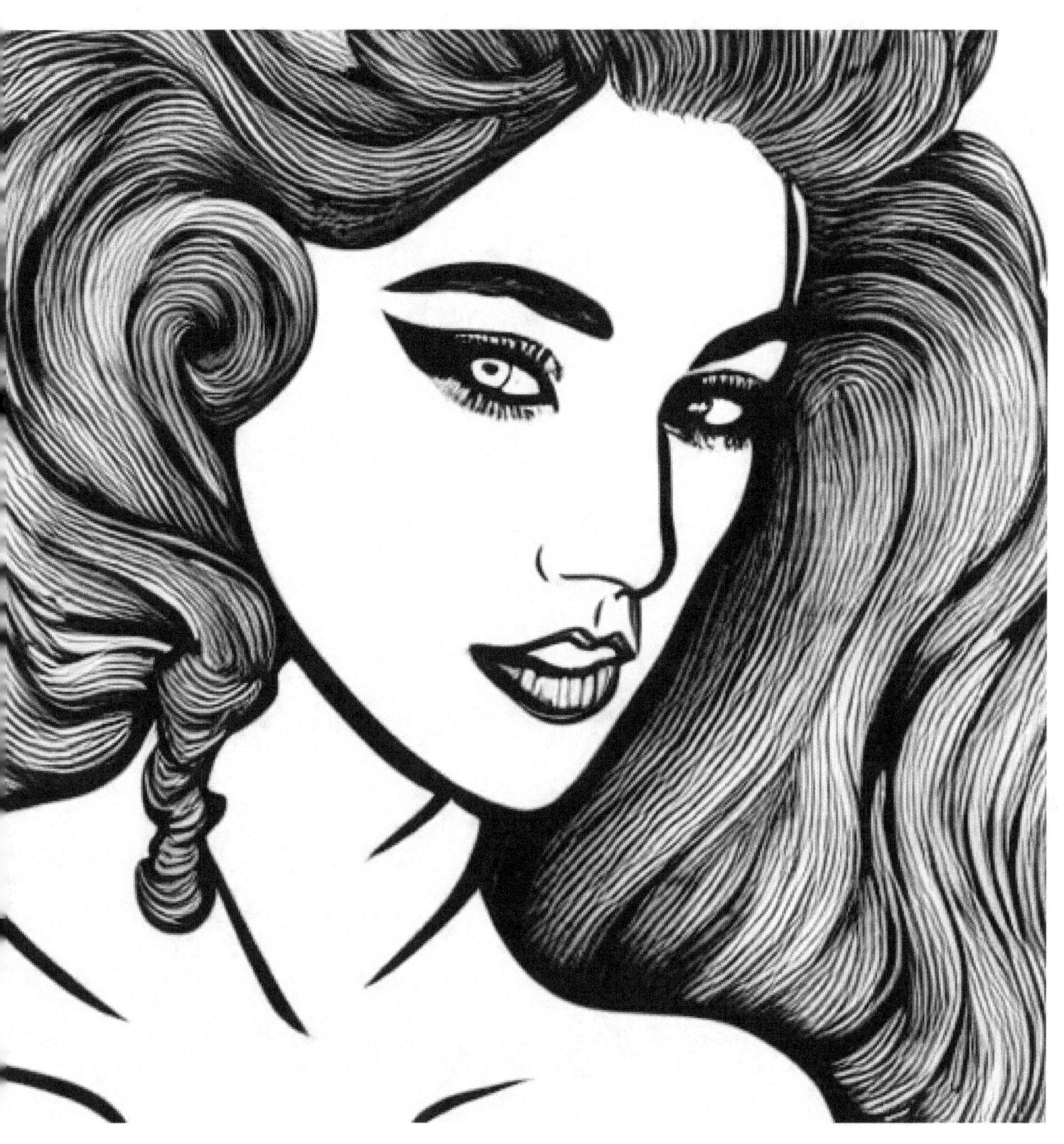

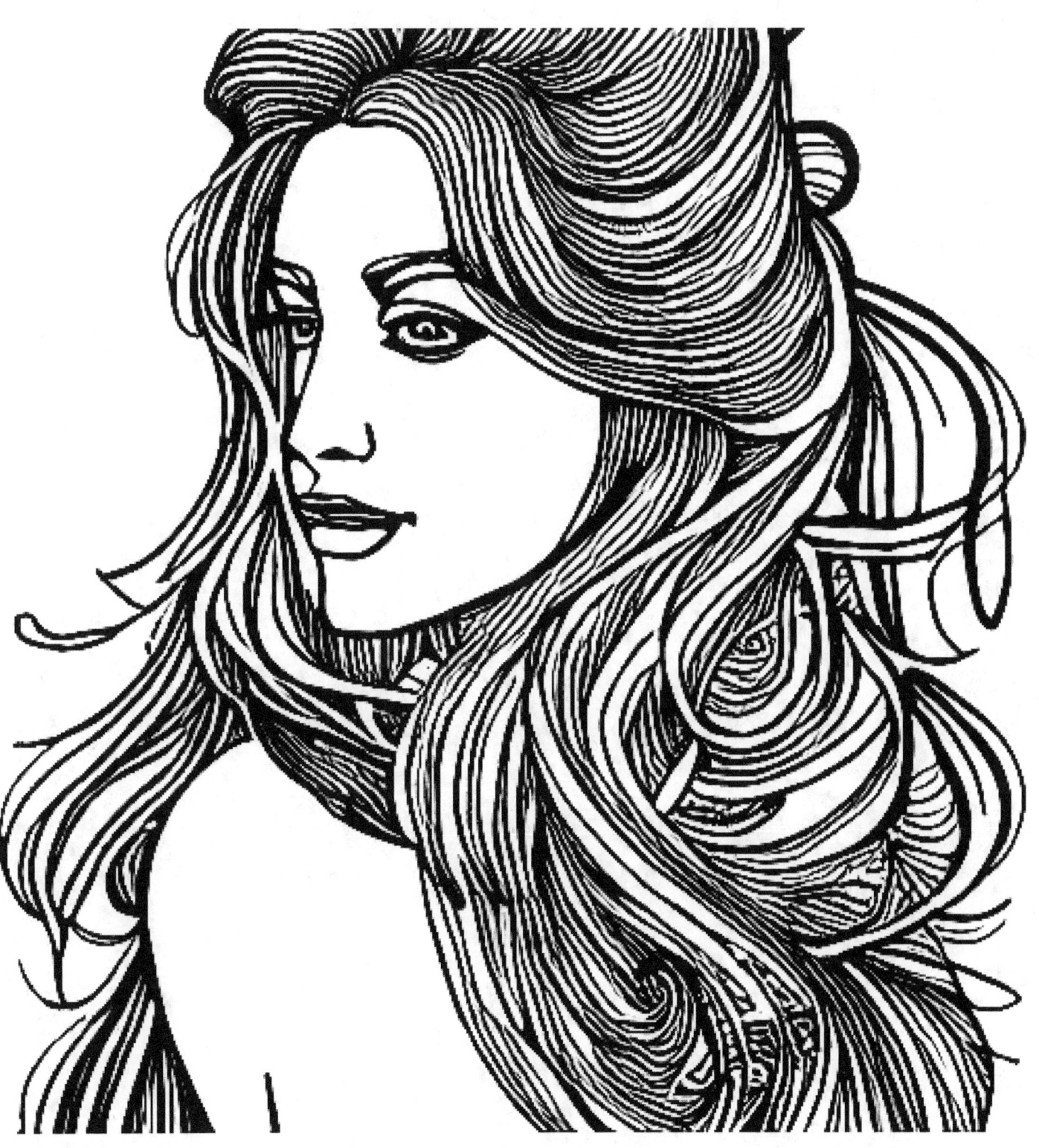

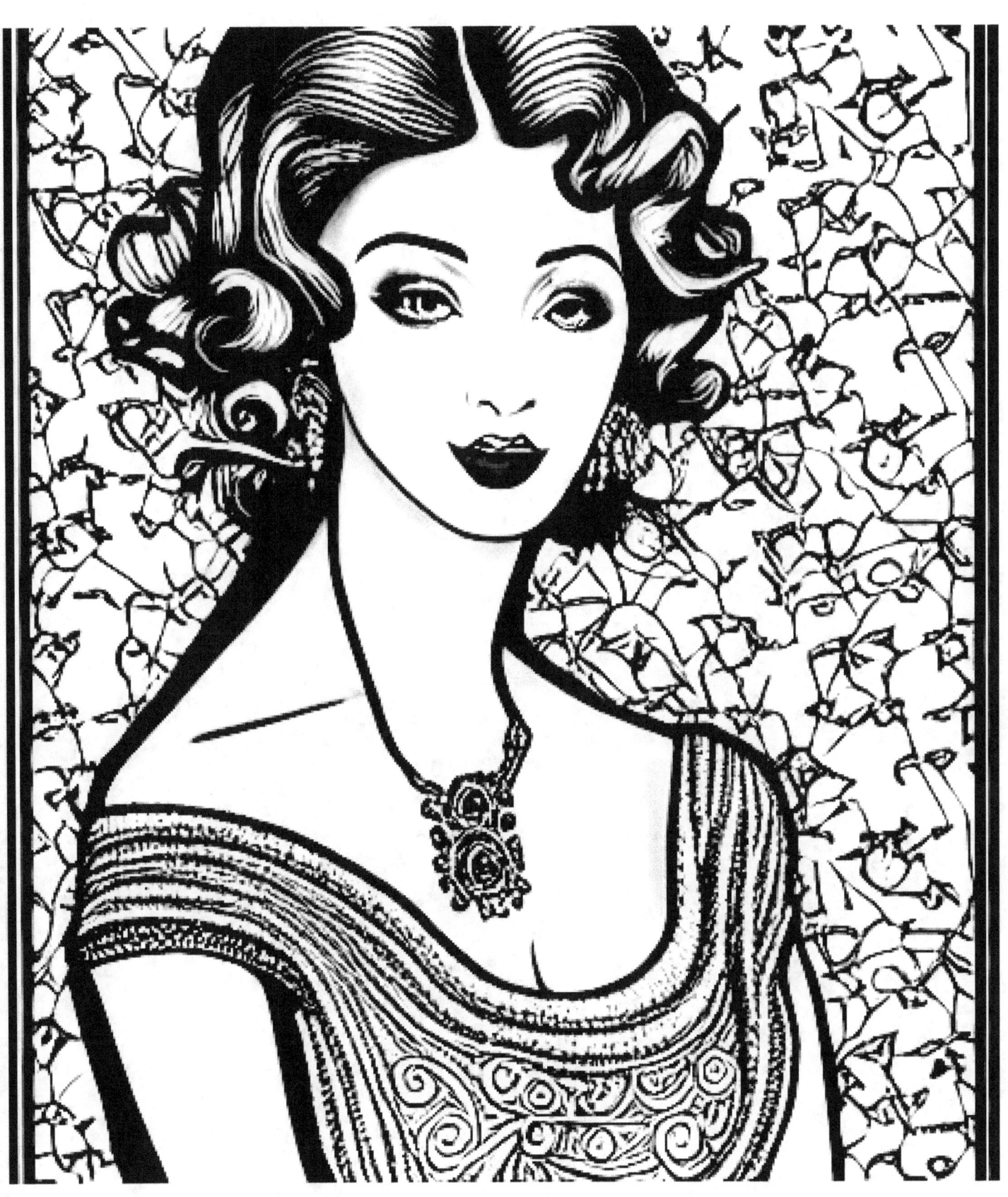

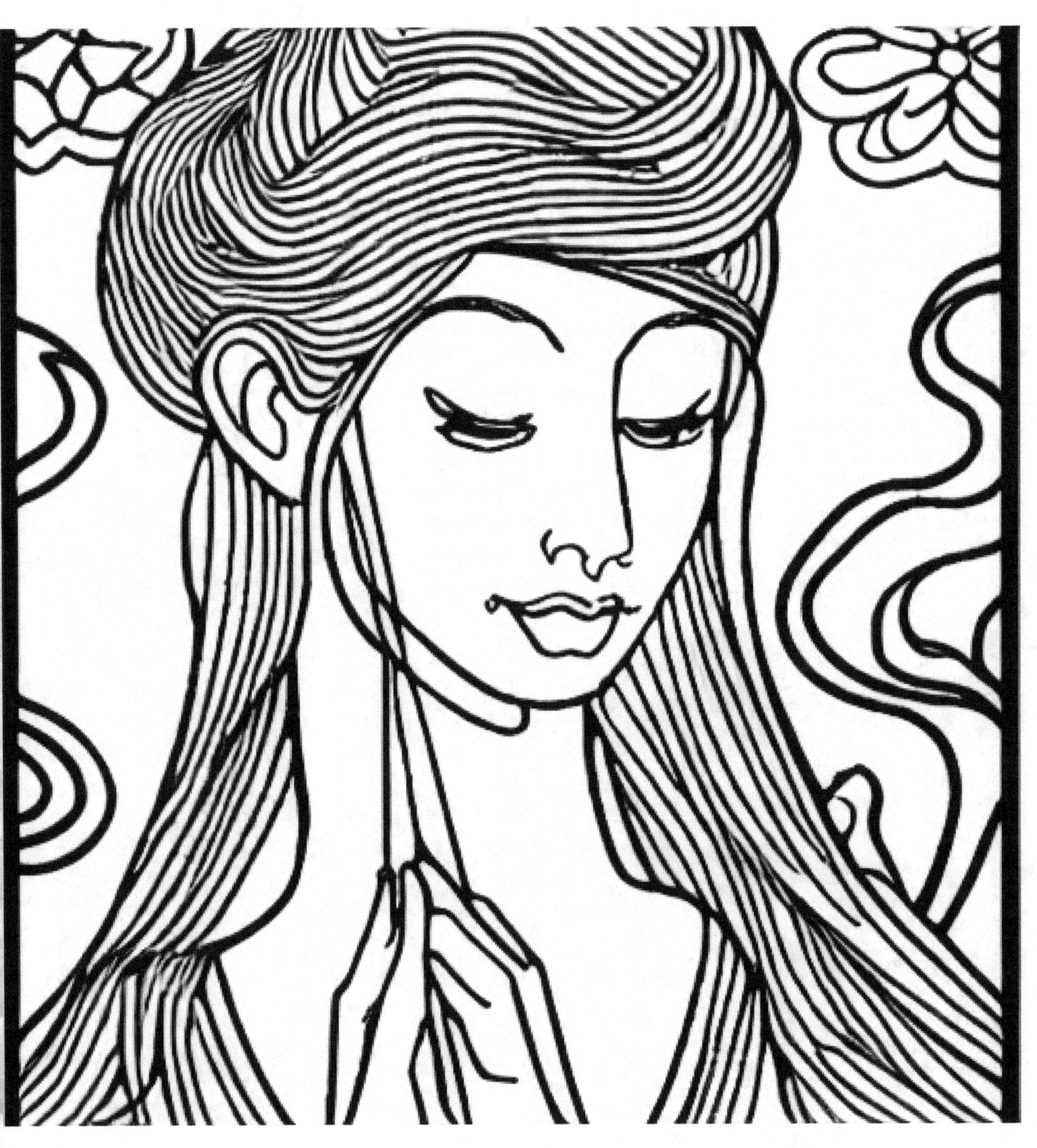

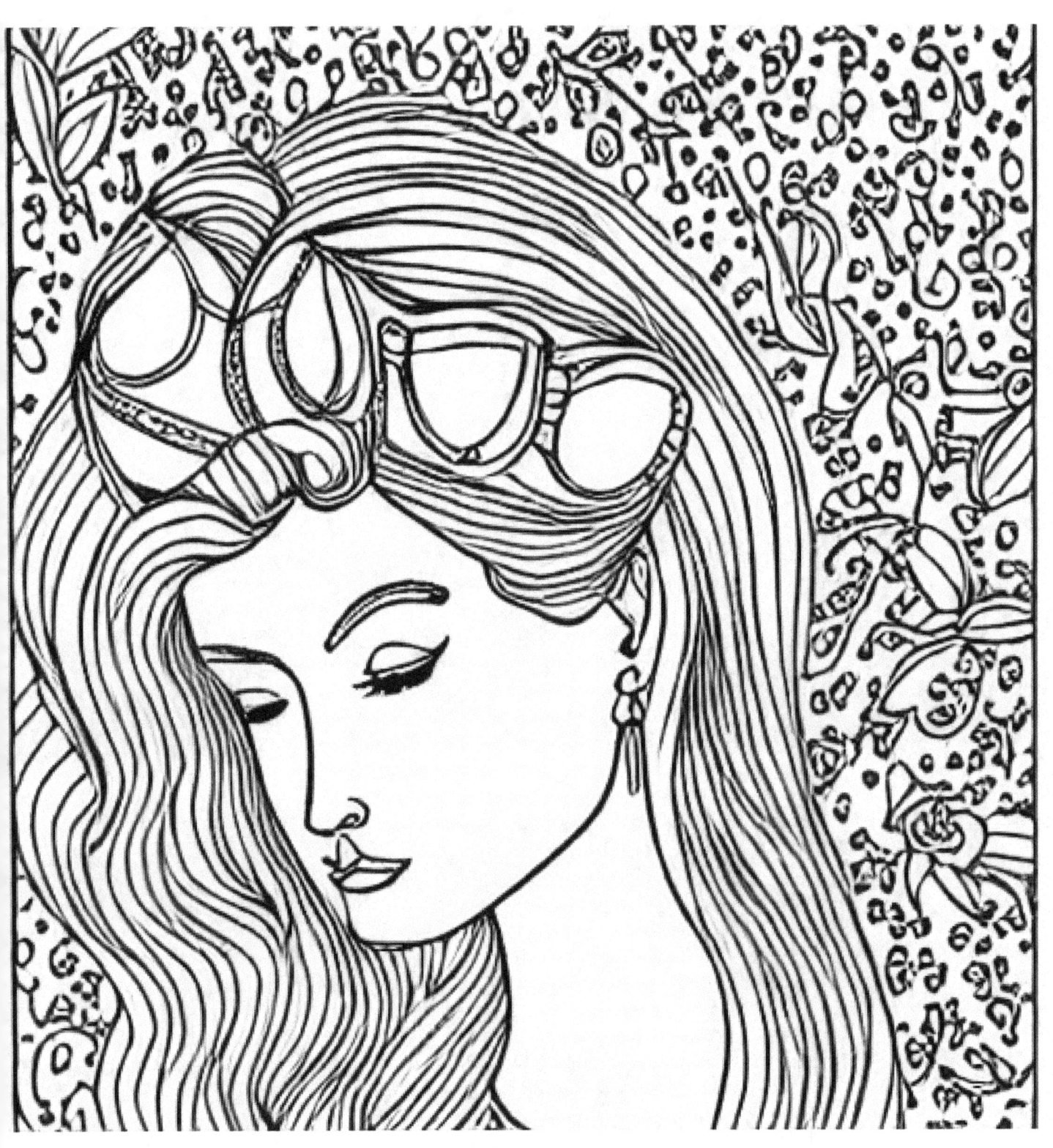

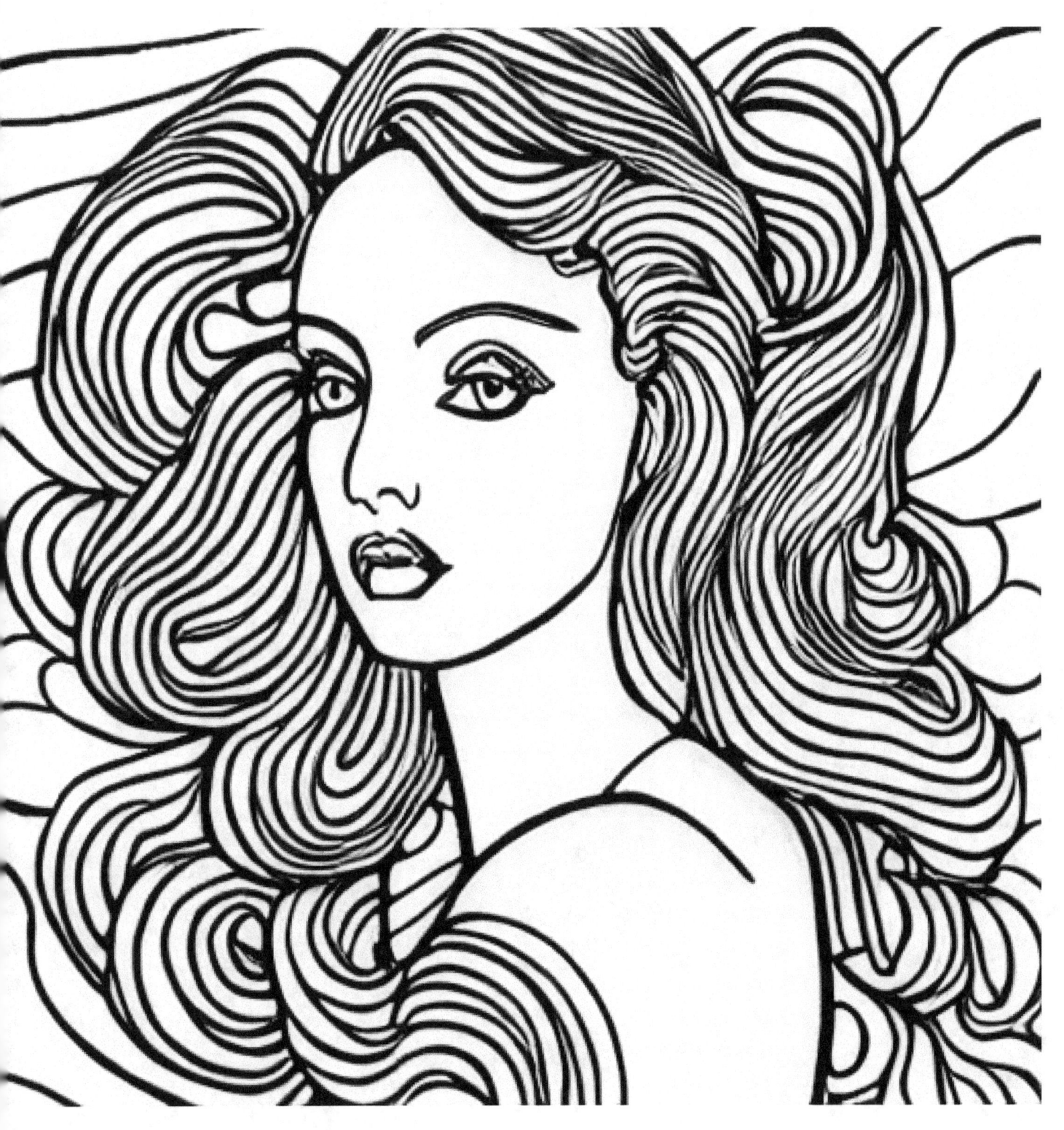

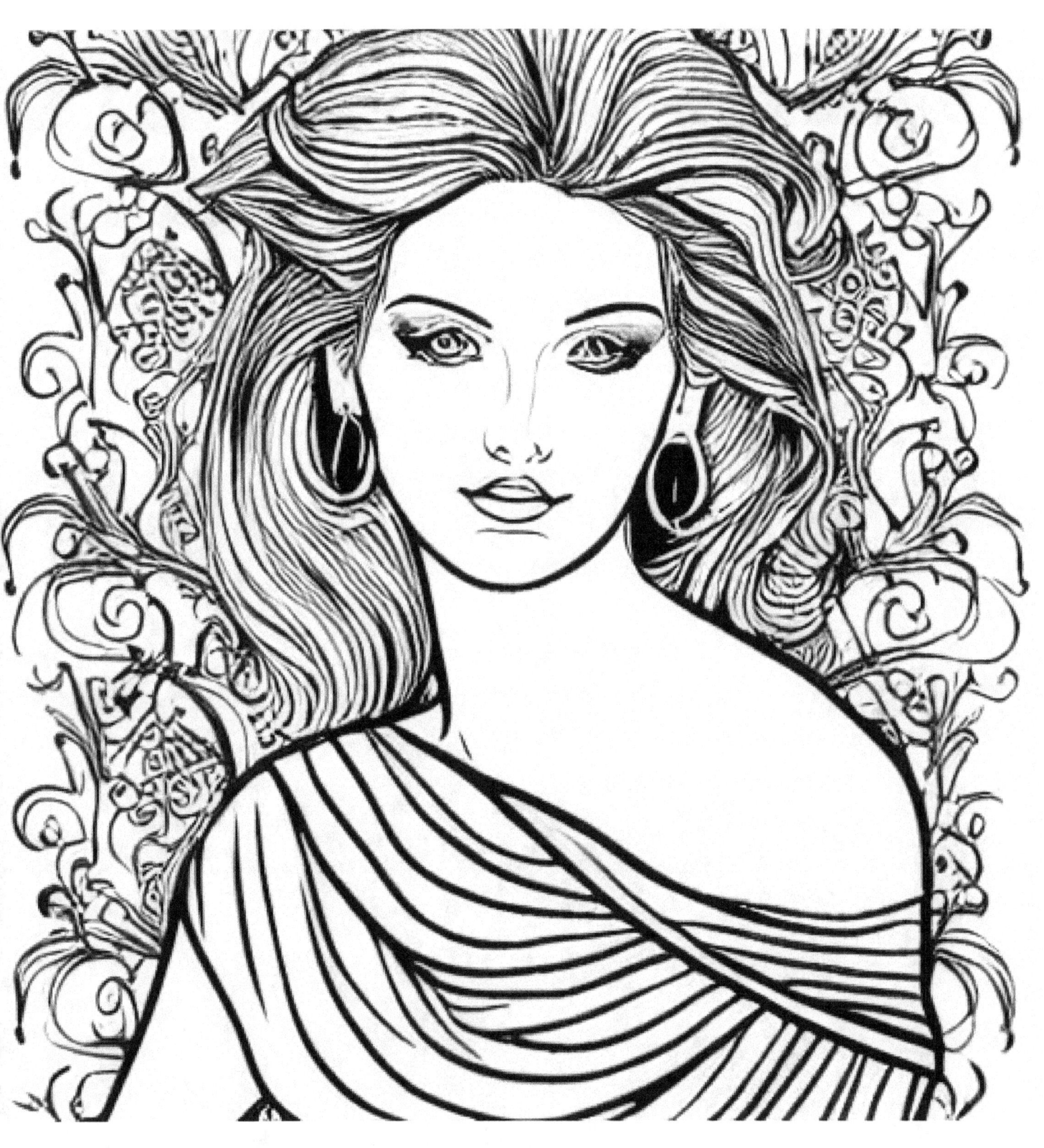

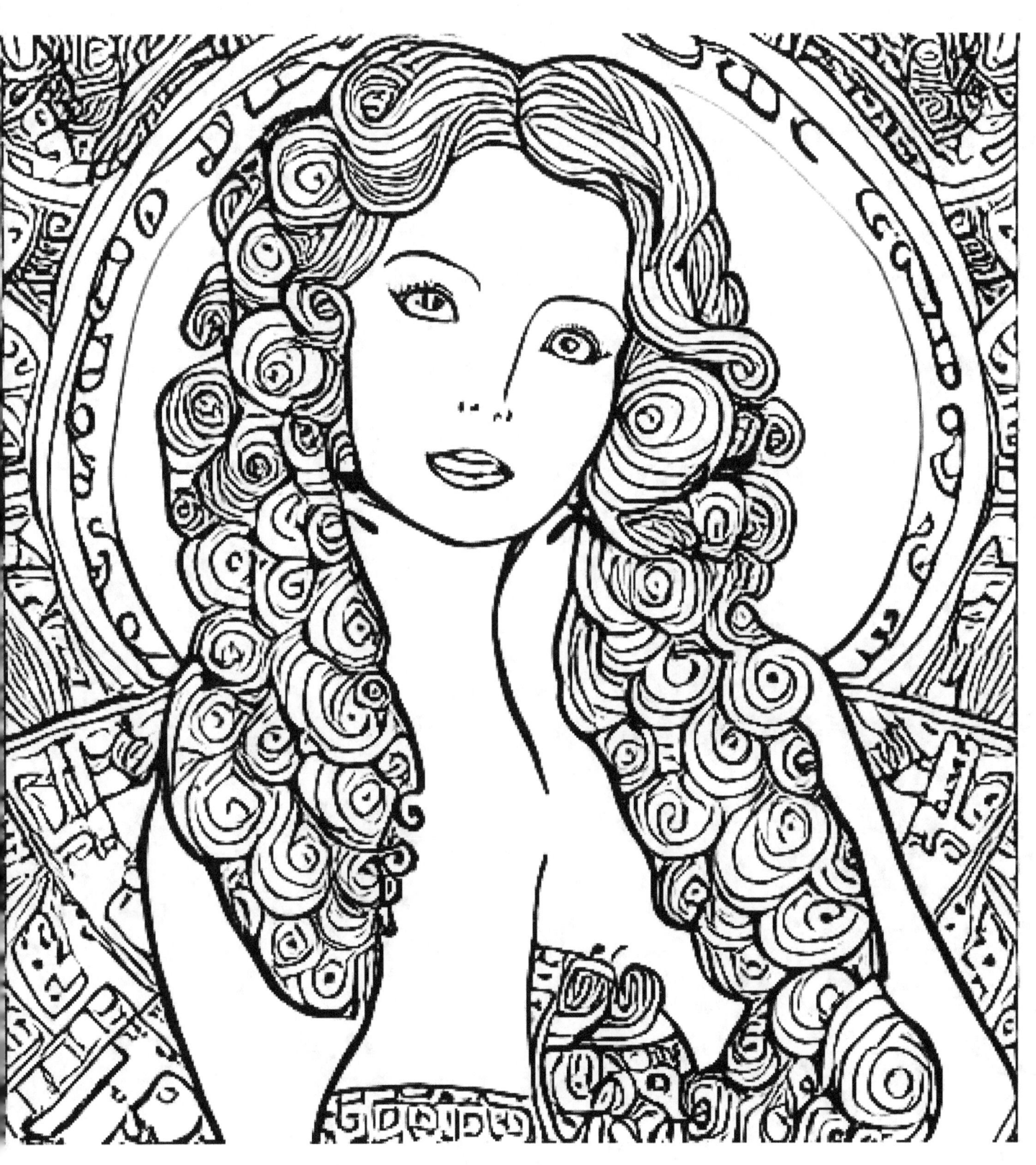

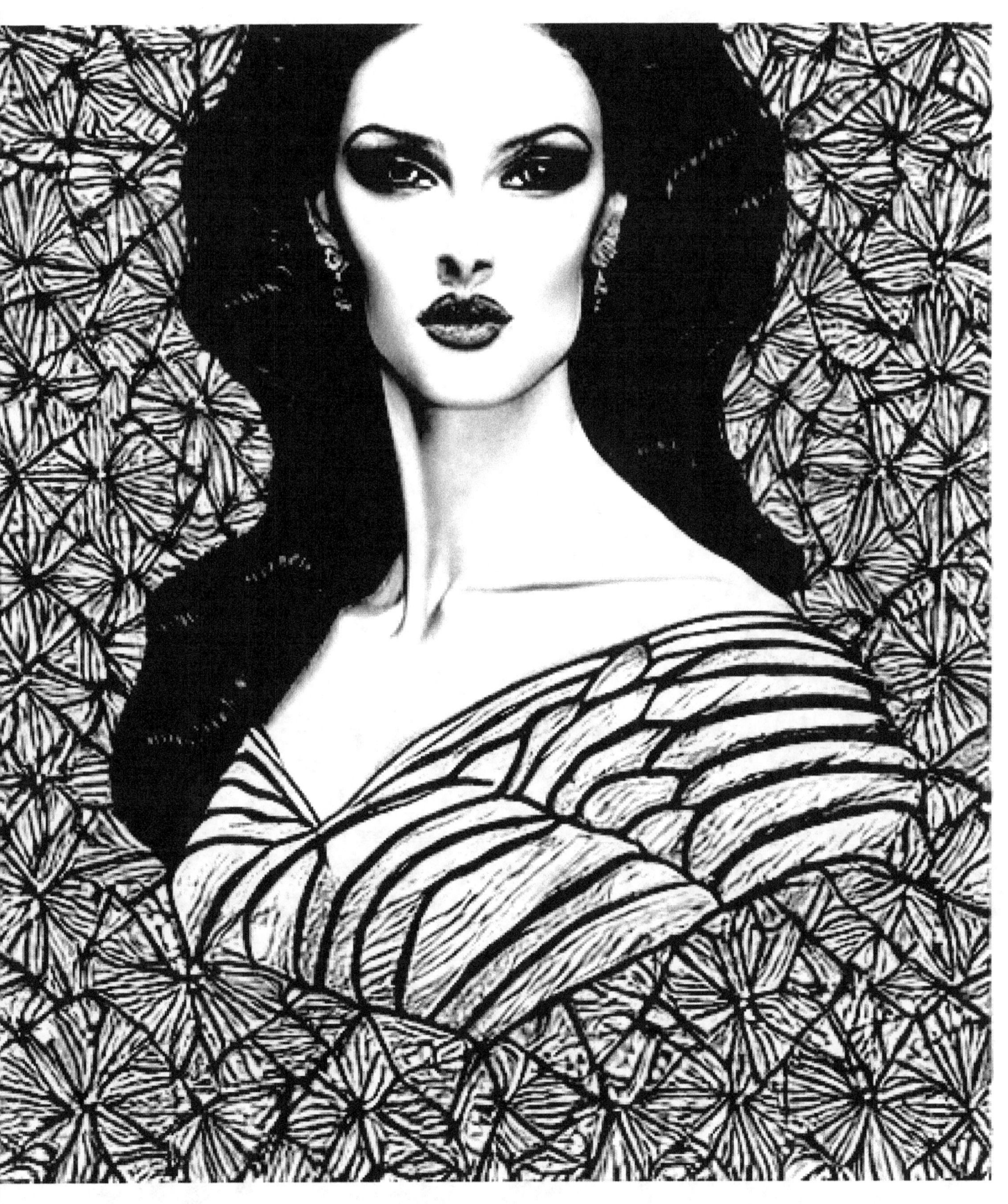

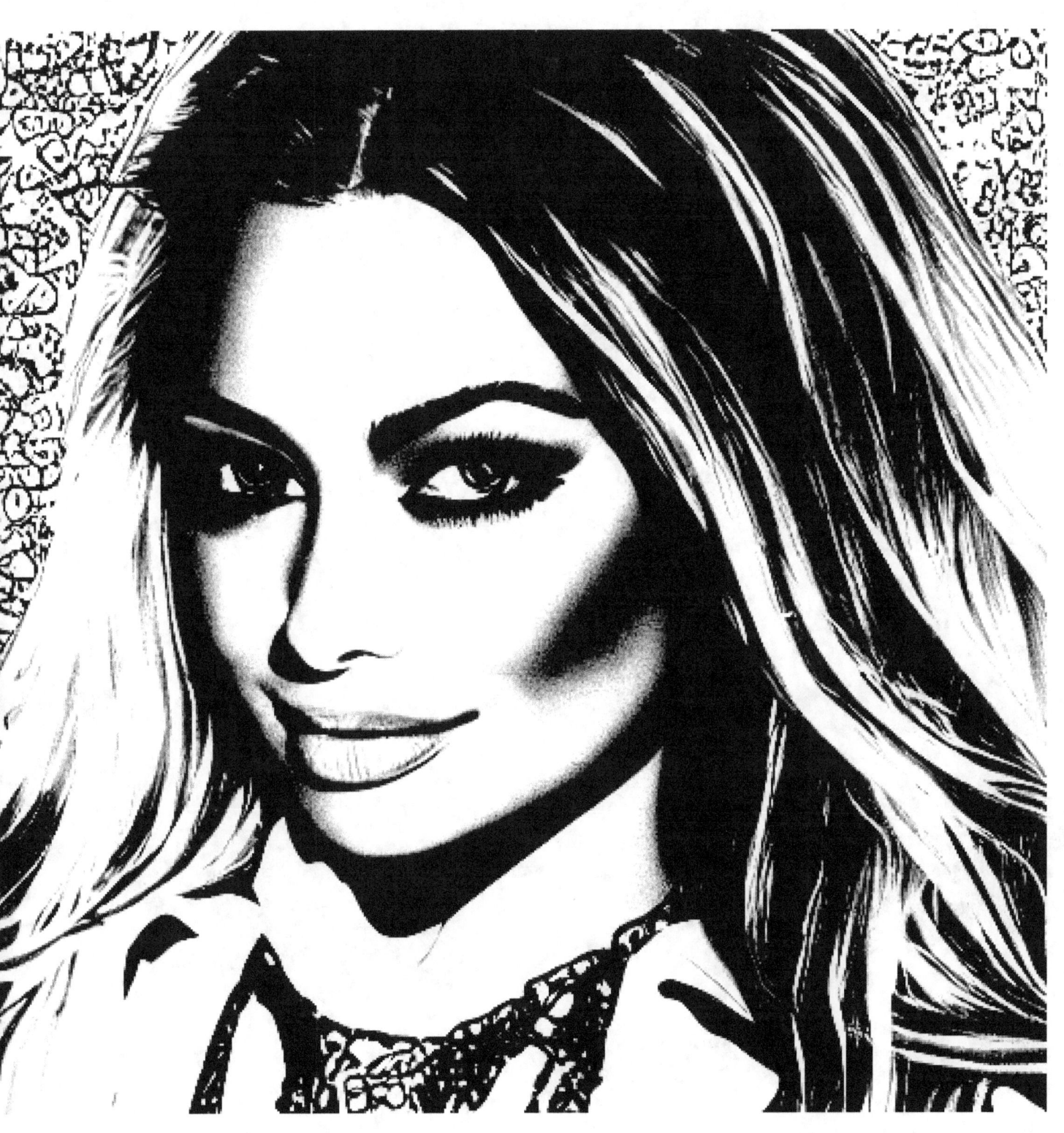

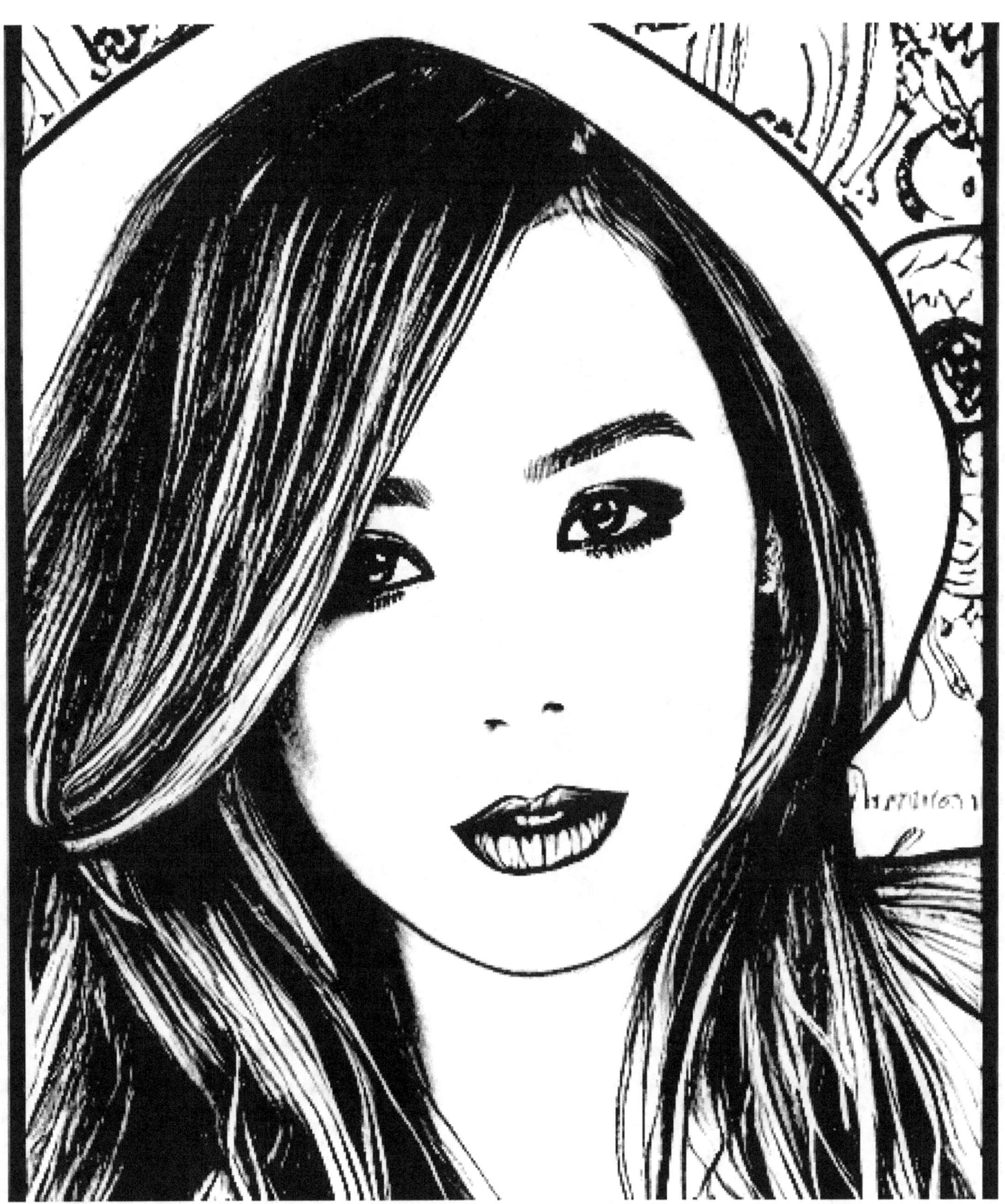

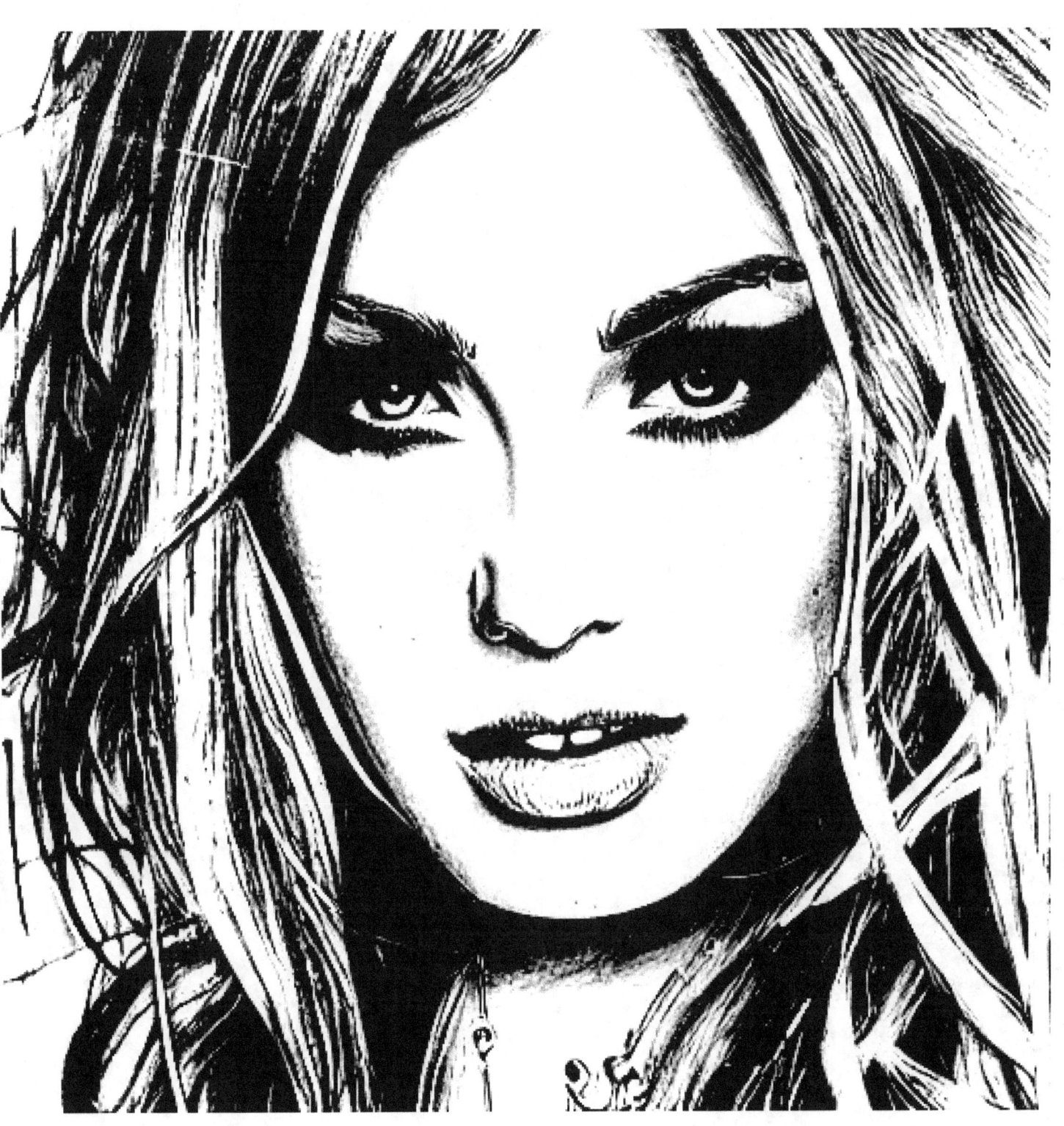

Beautiful women colouring book

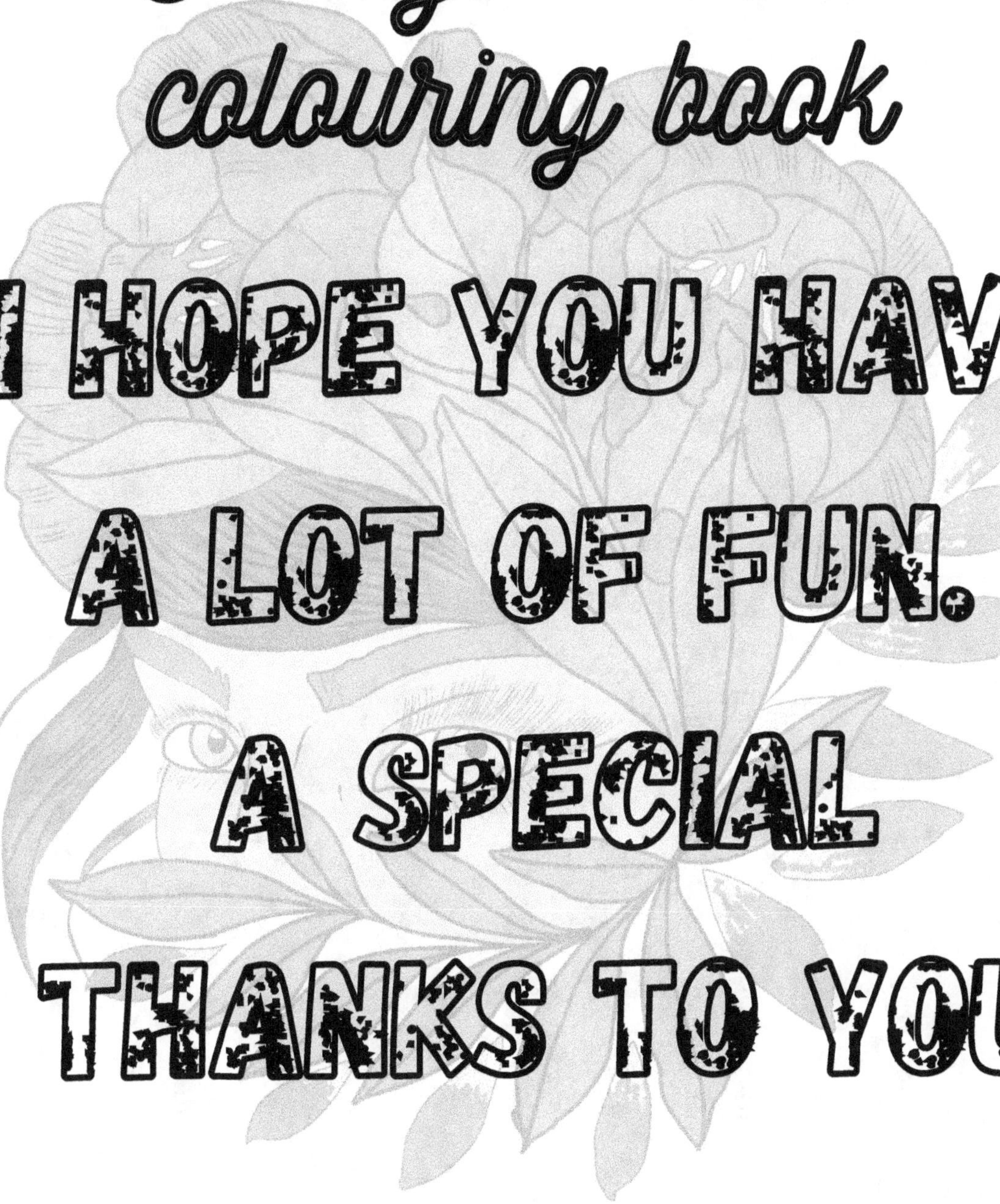

I HOPE YOU HAVE A LOT OF FUN.

A SPECIAL THANKS TO YOU

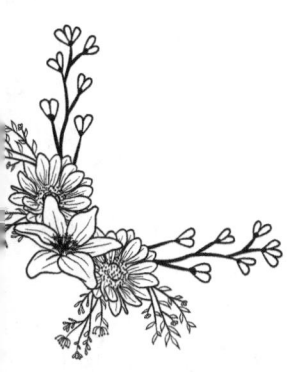
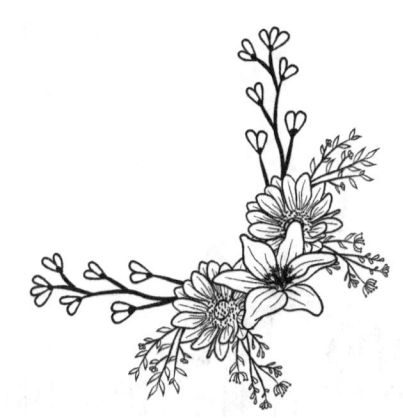